T0311817

BEING SUPERVISED

BEING SUPERVISED
A guide for supervisees

Erik de Haan and
Willemine Regouin

Routledge
Taylor & Francis Group

LONDON AND NEW YORK

Originally published in Dutch in 1991 (8th revised edition 2015) as *Supervisie, gids voor supervisanten* by Van Gorcum.

Originally published in English in 2017 by Karnac Books Ltd.

Published 2018 by Routledge
2 Park Square, Milton Park, Abingdon, Oxon OX14 4RN
711 Third Avenue, New York, NY 10017, USA

Routledge is an imprint of the Taylor & Francis Group, an informa business

British Library Cataloguing in Publication Data

A C.I.P. for this book is available from the British Library

ISBN-13: 9781782204237 (pbk)

Typeset by V Publishing Solutions Pvt Ltd., Chennai, India

CONTENTS

Part II Being on the supervisory journey

Part III Understanding the supervisory journey

ABOUT THE AUTHORS

Erik de Haan is a leadership and organisation development consultant, psychodynamic psychotherapist, executive coach and supervisor. He is the Director of the Ashridge Centre for Coaching and programme leader of the Ashridge Master's (MSc) in Executive Coaching, and the Ashridge Postgraduate Diploma (PG Dip) in Supervision. He was chair of the Association of Coaching Supervisors and non-executive board member of the Dutch Association for Supervision and Coaching. Erik is also Professor of Organisation Development & Coaching at the VU University of Amsterdam. He has written more than 150 articles and eleven books in different languages, among which are *Fearless Consulting* (2006), *Coaching with Colleagues* (2004, with Yvonne Burger), *Relational Coaching* (2008), *Supervision in Action* (2011), *Coaching Relationships* (2012, edited with Charlotte Sills), *The Leadership Shadow* (2014, with Anthony Kasozi), and *Management Pocketbook Team Coaching* (2016).

Willemine Regouin-van Leeuwen was a supervisor and educator of supervisors in Holland for many decades. Willemine also taught philosophy and published the first edition of this book in 1991.

INTRODUCTION

Much has already been written about supervision. But it is striking how much of this literature—both in the UK and internationally—is aimed principally at supervisors, policy makers, and others with a professional interest in supervision. The supervisee, the person who is receiving supervision and was the reason for starting it, is hardly ever addressed directly.[1]

This fact is remarkable; after all, what is a supervisor without a supervisee? Don't the two belong together, in the same way that teachers exist by virtue of students and the concept of parents would be unthinkable without referring to a child? But then, children's books were also "invented" relatively recently and are now impossible to live without. So, supervisees, bide your time: dawn is tingeing the horizon! In this book, we attempt to approach the main strands in supervision (theory, methodology, practice) from the "other" perspective: that of the supervisee.

Supervision is seen by many as an important option for further development and training, with particular use in converting insights and experience that have already been acquired into (more) professional competence. Supervision is especially important for jobs and professions that are client- (patient-, pupil-) oriented, where communication between the practitioner and one or more others plays an important role.

This guide for supervisees is based on the body of knowledge in these helping professions with a particular relational outlook. Supervisors appear to share a broad consensus on this, although there are shades of disagreement about the focus of supervision: is it just about the supervisee, or is there more to it?

In our view, supervision is about the meeting point between person and profession, as illuminated by the meeting point here and now, between two practitioners, supervisor, and supervisee(s). More precisely, it is about the supervisee and the quality of their performance in professional practice, within a social and socio-cultural context. It is from these perspectives that we have ourselves supervised and have written this book. We therefore define supervision as a didactic method focused on acquiring (more) personal competence to pursue client-oriented jobs, otherwise called "the helping professions", particularly where the relationship and/or interactions between the practitioner and those they are serving play an important role.

Relationship and interaction

- A *relationship* is a temporary or longer-term emotional connection between people in which experiences, insights, and feelings are exchanged. There are different types of relationship, such as personal relationships, which are an aim in themselves, and functional relationships, which are focused on an aim associated with their task, such as service provision, achieving contractual outcomes or nurturing a personal learning process. Supervision entails a functional relationship between supervisor and supervisee with the aim of achieving supervision objectives.
- *Interaction* is about actions between individuals, especially occasional or repeated exchanges of information, insights, and/or feelings between people who may or may not share a personal relationship. For example, telephone helplines involve interaction between the caller and the person taking the call, who usually do not know each other and have little or no contact beyond the call.

Objectives

The readers we had in mind initially as we wrote this book were students in higher professional education and experienced practitioners of helping professions where "helping" is a sensitive issue and a challenge in itself, such as social work, psychotherapy, education, and consultancy.

Since then (it is now twenty-five years after the first edition of this book) we have realised that other people could use and benefit from this guide as well, such as pupils in secondary vocational education, novice supervisors, and other professional facilitators and coaches, as well as practitioners in diverse sectors such as nursing, doctoring, and policing. However, this book is intended first and foremost for *supervisees*, as an information resource and a guideline. It can also serve as a refresher for former supervisees and supervisors themselves.

We try to show supervisees the ropes, to get them started on their forthcoming journey of (self-) discovery, which is probably causing them a degree of ambivalence, fuelled by uncertainty and insecurity. The metaphor of a journey is used to lighten the process of settling into supervision—which is no easy undertaking—and to make it more accessible to supervisees. Our own experience, as both a supervisee and a supervisor for a broad variety of supervisees, was the main source of inspiration for our writing. We also drew on the relevant available literature, despite it being written mainly for supervisors (whether experienced or in training).

Structure of this book

The shape of this guide reflects the supervisory process itself: the reader is introduced to the subject step by step. The spiral shape of learning in supervision can also be recognised: themes keep recurring, viewed from different perspectives and inviting further and hopefully deeper insights.

- Part I is a broad and yet concise exploration intended to inform, and to assist in introducing supervision to *future supervisees*. It concludes by inviting them to engage in an exercise.
- Part II is addressed to *novice supervisees* and examines the supervisory process on the basis of its three main stages. Themes from Part I

are looked at more closely and different topics are introduced. Part II concludes with an exercise and an example of how a writing problem (fairly common in supervision) was resolved.

- Part III is intended mainly for *advanced supervisees*. This part is a deeper philosophical exploration focused specifically on the relationship between the person and their profession. It concludes with some practical suggestions.

Besides the three sections addressed to future, novice and advanced supervisees, a fourth part could have been added to complete the picture. This is because there is a fourth category of supervisees: those who are in training to become supervisors and, as such, as novice supervisors, are receiving supervision of supervision ("SoS"). Supervision of supervision is not discussed in this book because there are already many books for supervisors. However, supervisors in training can still benefit from this book in imagining the concerns of their supervisees, as we have heard following the earlier editions.[2]

For each category of reader, we have made every effort to cite and attribute our sources correctly. For those who would like further information, and/or for the purposes of study, an up-to-date list of references has been added. A glossary of frequently used terms with brief descriptions is also included.

Part I

Starting the supervisory journey

Initial orientation, including getting started as a supervisee

Anyone going on a journey would do well to consider certain aspects in advance, such as the whys and wherefores of the trip, travelling companions, the Highway Code, any luggage needed, directions, and stops along the way.

Similarly, an orientation is crucial before undertaking the journey of discovery called "supervision", as this journey can and should have all sorts of unforeseen consequences.

Part I is intended for future supervisees and contains an initial broad exploration of questions surrounding the "why" of supervision, contractual rights and commitments, supervision as a learning process, and the critical, emotional aspects of learning in supervision sessions. Part I concludes with an exercise. The various stages and themes of supervision are then discussed in more detail.

1 Why supervision?

Supervision is a learning method for both novice and advanced practitioners of professions in which interaction between the worker and others plays an important role. These are professions also known as "the helping professions" (see, for example, Hawkins & Shohet, 2006). Supervision teaches professionals in those client- or person-oriented professions how to acquire and improve their professional competence, in a rather unique way that mirrors the professions themselves. Supervision is therefore itself also a "helping profession".

The supervisory process requires regular discussion of the supervisee's work experiences over a period of time, in such a way that learning and change become embedded in those work experiences. Supervision can take place individually or in small groups of up to eight colleagues from the same profession. Periods of supervision vary in length, from a one-off assignment related to a particular client involving very few sessions, to a series of weekly or biweekly sessions over several terms, or five to eight sessions a year for an experienced practitioner. Within the helping professions, supervisory contracts can be among the longest, stretching out over many years in some cases.

Although supervision generally begins as a key part of the professional training and practice in a particular helping profession, it will then become a specific practice requirement for most practitioners. Thus, supervision is increasingly being recommended for the entire duration of work in a helping profession—and not just at the outset when people are still in training. Many professional associations now require their members to be "in supervision" for a minimum number of sessions (usually four to six for part-time practitioners and up to ten for full-time clinical professionals) per year. The need for supervision can increase in times of transition, such as during company mergers and takeovers, when entering and mastering a new field of work, or before retirement.

1.1 Training

Professional training and qualification (both full time and part time) prepares students for a particular profession. In terms of content, this is normally done along three different paths that merge at the end:

a. general and profession-specific theory;
b. methodological principles, practices, and approaches;
c. practical skills.

For the student who wishes to learn the profession in question, this means acquiring:

a. Basic knowledge of people, their behaviour, and their interrelationships within a socio-cultural context. Plus, of course, acquiring knowledge about the profession and its working methods.
b. The right professional attitude, which students can develop through their methodology sessions and practical exercises. In these, they learn how to work within the profession and what options and choices they have within the profession. Students can also learn a variety of ways to see themselves in connection with their professional practice.
c. Finally, learning a wide range of skills provides students with a practical set of tools they can use when they actually get down to work in the profession. Training institutes often act as intermediaries in finding options for an initial introduction to practice, in the form of practical exercises, role-play and/or internships or temporary placements.

1.2 Practice

At a certain point in their training it is time for students to take the lessons they have learned to date and apply them "in practice": in a placement, in the workplace, in contracted work.

For some students, this can be their first direct confrontation with professional practice, for example if it is their first placement. For others, it can mean renewing a previous commitment, for example in an existing employment context or a follow-up placement during the same qualification programme. Whatever the case, the student is faced with the task of converting her recently gained or refreshed knowledge into professional action. And of course that is easier said than done!

Especially if this is a first placement, good preparation can help to ease the transition from theory to practice. Nevertheless, to some extent you may feel "thrown in at the deep end". But how can you do that if you are daunted or lacking in self-confidence? People often talk about the "shock of practice" experienced by new practitioners. Practice turns out to be quite different from what you had imagined from within the safe surroundings of college, lecturers, and fellow students. Now you need to stand on your own two feet, and feelings of loneliness, doubt or incompetence can creep up on you. The feeling does subside with time and habituation, but for now you just have to deal with it!

1.3 Supervision

To face their first (and later) problems in practice, practitioners can often rely on people responsible for placement and/or work practice, client coordination, care and team management, and on practical exercises with lecturers and fellow students during the "back in training" days.

But for practitioners who really want to develop their professional competence, all of this is not enough. The still-fragile new knowledge, professional stance, and competencies are not self-sufficient and when tested in practice many new challenges and questions emerge. The new professional "persona" you have acquired can make you feel uncertain and lead to confusion. All developing practitioners find, if they are honest with themselves, that core experiences in helping conversations remain badly understood by them, fragmented, and lacking in coherence. In this kind of situation, supervision can be felt as a welcome relief. Only in supervision you can learn to find your own coherent understanding and clarity. Supervision helps to link, order and coordinate your thoughts and ideas, your views and feelings, and your skills and actions. In the supervision literature, this is described as acquiring *integration at the first level*, that is, that of the person.

Although this can be quite a job in itself, learning for your profession requires even more: thinking, feeling, reflecting, desiring and acting should be coordinated not only with each other but also with your functioning within the profession, notably in your specific work situations with clients. This is termed acquiring *integration at the second level*: the profession.

Professional identity

Clearly, the person and their profession are closely interrelated but there are tensions because as a professional you have to "act" a role and "act" it well. Supervision moves within the field of tension between these two poles: how you experience yourself (your personal identity) and how you experience yourself-with-clients (your professional identity). Moreover, these poles are constantly shifting during training and development. For young people still in their adolescence, the search for a personal identity is often ongoing. Mature professionals also wrestle with issues around identity, particularly when challenged by their clients or during major transitions in their lives.

Everyone, whatever their stage of life, faces the task of finding or redefining a professional identity. The supervisor can help by exploring with the supervisee the possibility of finding a new balance of her own.

Definition

In a nutshell, and to avoid possible misunderstandings, we offer the following definition:

- Supervision is not case management, care coordination, or team and practice leadership (these are focused on your functioning and performance in your work context).
- Supervision is also not coaching, mentoring, or consultation (requesting help with a challenge at work, possibly on a recurring basis).
- Nor is supervision a form of mental training, fitness, mindfulness, counselling, or psychotherapy (these provide help with personal balance and development).
- Supervision is not a type of skills training, although people do acquire more (professional) competence as a result of supervision.
- Supervision is not the same as peer consultation or action learning (these are group-based learning in practice with colleagues).

Instead, supervision is the key platform for helping practitioners to connect what they learn in theory with what they learn and do in practice, and is therefore at the core of all continuing professional development. Supervision can be defined as *disciplined reflection-in-relation wherein case history and principles are transformed into new potential for action and skills* (after Rapoport, 1954). Supervision is therefore a process in which new practical knowledge is generated while taking account of (ethical) principles. Practical knowledge is nothing other than an "irreversible change in potential actions" for the practitioner.

To put it concisely and simply, supervision is a useful aid that can help you to learn from your own experiences and practise your job or profession independently and in a more personalised way.

Case example

A supervision group of six comes together after just having participated in three days of training. One of the first to speak says he feels "issued out" as he dealt with all of his experiences and queries during the workshop. The second participant says, "well I do have a question: how do I handle the differences between my training clients (provided by the institution) and my new external clients who are beginning to come in". "Oh well, that in fact is a question of mine too", says the first speaker, "so there is something to work on for me too." The third participant says, "I am an outcomes-focused person, I always want to add value, and I think it interferes with my accepting my clients as they are. I want to maintain more 'creative indifference' when I work with them." The fourth participant says, "I would like the group to help me to understand what would enable me to work less directively with my clients." With some guidance from the supervisor, the group decides to work with these three questions and assign some forty-five minutes to each. The first two speakers start out in a pair to work on the second speaker's query ("How can we handle differences between training clients and new, paying clients?") after which they receive feedback from the rest of the group. The group has already met some five times before, so the supervisor leans back as group members give each other helpful, constructive feedback. At the end they are all surprised and excited that there was still so much to learn straight after those intensive training days, and they ask the supervisor if they could stay together longer than the initially contracted eight sessions.

2 Contracting: the way to monitor your progress

If supervision has been decided on, the supervisee is entitled to receive it from a competent supervisor—preferably one who is qualified and registered. Both supervisee and supervisor commit themselves to doing everything they can to get the supervision off to a good start and to bring it to a satisfactory conclusion. The foundation for this is a basic contract (see for example the standard supervision contract in Appendix A), ideally drawn up in writing. The contracting parties are the sponsor, the supervisor, and the supervisee(s).

Before supervision properly begins, several conditions need to be met, the most important of which are:

1. Agreement between sponsor, supervisor, and supervisee regarding the formal objective(s) of the supervision.
2. The existence of relevant work for the supervisee (as part of for example, placement, or employment), to allow the necessary link between learning and working.
3. Broad agreement on the time frame for supervision, as well as the number, frequency, place and duration of individual sessions.
4. Agreement on any reporting to be done to the sponsor, with or without an assessment of performance.
5. Agreement on material and organisational matters such as the supervisor's fee, terms of cancellation, availability of a suitable and accessible workspace.
6. The right supervisory combination: which supervisor works with which supervisee(s) and who makes that decision? Do supervisees or supervisors have any say? Have any contraindications been specified? Why is the choice being made for either individual or group supervision sessions?
7. Agreement on the ethical principles and code of conduct to serve as the basis for supervision.[1] What options are available in the event of a conflict between supervisor and supervisee that cannot be resolved by mutual agreement? Ideally there should be an appeal procedure.

2.1 Contracting with the organisational sponsor

There are various types of sponsor who can prescribe or recommend supervision and with whom the conditions can be negotiated: they include professional training institutes, professional associations, clinics and NHS or care institutions, and supervisees organising their own supervision. Unless supervision is self-referred or overlooked by a professional association, the supervisor has to contract twice in principle: once with the sponsor for a framework contract and once with the supervisee for a supervisory contract.

a. Supervision commissioned by a training or qualifying institution

Supervision can be offered either during initial training or as part of continuing education. Here, supervision is included in the contract between the institute and the students participating in the course. The (future) supervisees know where they stand from the outset: supervision is a compulsory part of their training and the supervision results will normally be assessed as good, satisfactory or unsatisfactory. There is usually an employment contract or other permanent framework contract between the institute and the supervisors.

b. Supervision commissioned by a professional care institution, clinic, or consultancy

Here too, there may be an employment contract and/or a general framework contract with supervisors. However, this is often not the case. If not, a supervision contract has to be negotiated with the client on each occasion. This is where double or triple contracting is most explicit: the employer offers an employee supervision and contracts agreements with both the employee and a supervisor. Once they have agreed on the basics, supervisor and future supervisee make detailed arrangements regarding the specific work they are to do together. Supervision for a supervisee/employee is therefore less straightforward than for a supervisee in training. However, usually there is no assessment as part of the supervisory contract, which simplifies matters.

So, before supervision can begin, sponsor and supervisee first need to agree on whether or not to go ahead. And if they do: why, when, to what end, for how long, under what conditions and with which supervisor?

c. Supervision commissioned by the supervisee

Here, the supervisee approaches a supervisor and organises a period of supervision on their own account (and often at their own expense), possibly through an intermediary. Private arrangements of this type involve only two contracting parties: the (future) supervisee and a supervisor. But here too, the conditions are negotiated with the supervisor in advance or during the first session, avoiding the need to deal with these matters during supervision itself.

2.2 Contracting between supervisor and supervisee

Once sponsor, supervisor and supervisee(s) have reached agreement on the basic contract and formal conditions, the substantive contracting on the actual content of the supervision can begin. This usually starts with the supervisee or group of supervisees initiating a first meeting with the supervisor. The first encounter is followed by one or more introductory sessions in which the participants attempt to reach provisional agreement on various matters. Known as supervisory contracting, this process concerns both the *objectives towards* and the *conditions under* which the parties will work together. These discussions conclude with a set of detailed arrangements concerning time and place, types of work contributions, contingencies in the event of illness or force majeure, and so on.

Conditions

Aside from the basic contract and other formal conditions, the other conditions are mainly relational. They concern the parties' willingness to work together, their ability to trust each other, their readiness and efforts to create and utilise an appropriate learning environment, and their respect for each other's individuality and personal integrity. Co-supervisees are expected to show a degree of loyalty: they must be willing to help each other as they learn during supervision, and to work together to address challenges. It is also a good idea to make arrangements to protect each other's privacy, that is, to handle personal information carefully. This also applies to the privacy of clients and other parties featuring as "learning material" in discussions of casework.

Finally, detailed arrangements are needed regarding the following (again, see Appendix A):

- date, time, and place of supervision sessions;
- working methods, contributions, type of casework or work contributions;
- interim evaluation(s), and how to change objectives, agreements and working methods where needed;
- the final evaluation and any assessment of the results achieved, including final reporting.

Objectives

If all of these matters are discussed thoroughly at the start of supervision, a realistic learning environment can be created. The supervision partners can refer to their existing arrangements, and each partner knows where they stand. They can put into place a mutual understanding of objectives in working together, which will entail a review of case work and also usually some more personal longer-term objectives for the supervisee (such as "a better work-life balance", "developing my ability to teach and/or publish in the professional field", "developing a more relational stance with my clients", etc.).

Nevertheless, even with thorough contracting on all these levels, many important aspects will remain undiscussed because they are as yet unknown or have not been made explicit. There are always implicit expectations during supervision, in addition to the explicit, contracted ones, especially regarding the supervisory process and the expected outcomes. This is often referred to as the *psychological contract*: "all that belongs in the contract but we have not made explicit, let alone put down on paper", that is, a collection of unwritten expectations between parties working together (Rousseau, 1995). The psychological contract between supervision partners can lead to disappointment: expectations have been created but it is not clear how to fulfil them. Not only that, but the confidential and vulnerable nature of supervision can lead all too easily—and despite good contracting—to disappointment, personal antipathy, and conflict.

At the start of supervision, it is useful to have some understanding of how sensitive supervision feels, how much courage it takes to do it properly, and how much tolerance and even forgiveness are needed in order to get a relationship back on track after disappointments or ruptures. Hence the following section.

2.3 Dealing with disappointment and mustering courage

Years of research are gradually revealing the extent to which supervisees can struggle, even though supervision sessions are designed first and foremost for their benefit and even though supervision's main purpose is to further their work on their own competences, professional development and career. We now know from confidential, off-line interviews with supervisees that they are by no means always satisfied about their supervision. And worse, they sometimes take away very bad memories from supervision, they report that they have often felt out in the cold alone, or were less open as they felt compelled to protect themselves or their supervisor in some way.[2]

As many as thirty-eight per cent of the 158 supervisees (trainee clinical psychologists) surveyed by Moskowitz and Rupert (1983) reported conflict within their supervision relationship. Eighty-four per cent of those had been forced to raise the matter themselves, either because their supervisor had been unaware of the conflict or had not reviewed it or brought it up for discussion. Conflicts centred on supervision "style" were easier to resolve than conflicts caused by a clash of personality. If conflicts were not resolved, the supervisees adjusted their behaviour: they sought help from others, they became less open and concealed their professional struggles and queries, while they dutifully did what their supervisor asked of them but without it really affecting their clinical work. Numerous other empirical studies show that supervisees do not bring their most pertinent issues to supervision, sometimes for fear that the process will be too painful or shaming for themselves, sometimes related to an experience of awe or a need to shield their supervisor—and themselves—from sensitive issues or potential conflict (Lawton, 2000). This applies also to experienced practitioners and even to supervisors themselves (see for example Day, De Haan, Sills, Bertie, & Blass, 2008). Time after time the literature shows that during the process of supervision supervisees expect more empathy, listening ability and support from their supervisors than they feel they receive (Gray, Ladany, Walker, & Ancis, 2001).

With hindsight, these research results do not seem so strange. Most supervision is still compulsory, whether organised in a training context, within a professional institution, or to meet membership requirements imposed by a professional association (e.g. "a minimum of six individual supervision sessions per year"). In the majority of cases, therefore, there is an element of compulsion or at least obligation. Moreover, in many cases, for example where supervision is organised by a training institute or an employer, the supervisee cannot choose their own supervisor. If we also consider the fact that, as a supervisee, you are expected to put your cards on the table, to contribute the case material that causes you the greatest anxiety or uncertainty and, especially, to discuss your own doubts and faults openly with your supervisor, it is not surprising that supervisees often have negative experiences in or around supervision. Add to this the fact that the supervisor has a lot of power, often gives opinions—including written evaluations—and even, in some cases, plays a role in deciding whether a supervisee can continue to train or to practise in their profession, and the thirty-eight per cent of supervision relationships that Moskowitz and Rupert (1983) found to involve conflict appears to be on the low side.

Group supervision has the additional complication that supervisees are required to work together. Have they chosen each other? Do they actually like each other? Do they see each other as peers and "comrades in adversity"? There will invariably be times when their peer relationships are put to the test, as well as their relationships with their supervisor. They have somehow to divide up their allotted supervision time between them, and they sometimes feel that someone else is receiving more attention or being treated more favourably.

In addition, they have to maintain helping relationships with each other: relationships in which ambivalence, wavering trust, and fragile security always play a significant role. And even if all of that is going well, they can come up against different levels of competence, ambition, and success within the group, which can trigger feelings of jealousy or superiority, or make them feel (temporarily) unwelcome in the group.

Supervisees often feel shame during supervision; they feel vulnerable and insecure, and they feel exposed, especially after painful feedback or criticism from the supervisor—or if they have stuck their necks out and expressed criticism of their own. It is not unusual to feel nervous or hesitant before embarking on supervision, or to feel upset, exhausted, confused, offended, or stripped bare afterwards.

However, in our view these common negative feelings are no reason not to take part or to be reticent about supervision. We believe that it is precisely *because of* these uncertainties and sensitivities that so much can be learned in supervision. Provided you also feel a "minimum of trust" that the supervisor has your best interests at heart, tensions can yield a lot of benefits. Our advice is therefore to keep "exposing" yourself as much as possible and to contribute truly sensitive case material, even if you have doubts about your supervisory relationship, because this can be ultimately very fruitful. Moreover, you in turn are probably dealing with ambivalence, tension, or (veiled) opposition on the part of your clients, end-users or students, and you are in many cases likewise trying to help people who are not fully committed or have not had full authority in choosing you. So if you can apply yourself to supervision and continue to learn despite tensions and irritations, you will have more chance of being of service in your own helping conversations with other people who are not altogether dissimilar from you as you are in supervision.

We ourselves have learned a great deal through working with supervisors we had not had a hand in choosing, and even with supervisors we had initially looked down on or felt an urge to protect. To put it succinctly, it is precisely the sensitive case material and the sensitive relationship that teaches the most valuable lessons. At the same time, of course, it is good to be prepared for tensions and sensitivities in the hope of persevering despite vulnerability while continuing to develop forgiveness and acceptance, both for yourself and for your supervisor.

Moskowitz and Rupert (1983) found that there were three main types of conflict that arise in supervision:

1. Conflicts related to theoretical orientation

It is entirely possible to be assigned to a supervisor with a different theoretical orientation, or to discover that ideological differences are getting in the way of supervision. This is somewhat ironic: we know from quantitative research that theoretical differences in approaches and models do not significantly influence the effectiveness of helping conversations (see De Haan, 2012; Appendix B). Indeed, we can learn a great deal from differences in perspective, theoretical or otherwise, so it is probably beneficial to have worked with supervisors having a variety of theoretical leanings. On the other hand, there may be times when your supervisor becomes entrenched in an ideological position that strikes you as dogmatic, or lays down ethical boundaries that you do not recognise or see as absolute. Here, it is best to remain open to your supervisor's perspective while at the same time having the courage to stand up for your own views within the context of a hopefully strong underlying relationship. The ideal scenario, of course, is one where supervisor and supervisee are able to explore their different positions and come to the joint realisation that both are valid and mostly say something about their own personalities, educational backgrounds or the different contexts in which they operate.

The history of helping conversations contains many examples of "rifts" between practitioners due to theoretical differences. In our view, this is not worth getting upset or estranged about. Our advice is to continue to differentiate between a theoretical "rift" and a personal "rift": the latter is often unnecessary when parties are at odds over theory.

At the extreme end, if both parties are so firmly wedded to their theoretical convictions that open and fresh reflection is inhibited, it is sometimes best to change supervisor if at all possible.

2. Conflicts related to supervision style

Styles do differ, of course. For example, you might feel safer with a more formal supervisor who continues to address you formally than with a more relaxed type who starts out on a first-name basis. A supervisor can come across as too forceful, too vague and unstructured, too businesslike and unsupportive, or too probing or similar to a therapist. Up to a point, it can be interesting to go along with your supervisor's style: just like differences in ideology, these differences in style can teach you a lot more. But if you start to feel inhibited, it may be worth saying something about this. Don't forget that you as the supervisee can participate in negotiating the supervisory contract. You can collaborate to find a style that suits your supervisor and is also acceptable to you. With time, you may notice your own needs in terms of style beginning to shift: you may for example, have appreciated a strict, businesslike, formal style at the outset but later develop a growing need for a two-way conversation, a shared quest and a different type of firmness.

3. Conflicts due to disruption in the relationship and personality clashes

Relationship problems are perhaps both the most common and the most intractable conflicts in supervision. When learning matters and casework dilemmas are critical, and the conversation is teetering right on the edge, it is easy for irritations to arise that cannot be resolved straight away. Irritation often stems from uncertainty or misunderstanding and, because supervisor and supervisee do not immediately realise what is happening, the situation gradually begins to escalate. Triggers are sometimes the tiniest things, such as forgetting an appointment or getting the time wrong, failing to do your "homework", not quite understanding the purpose of supervision, displaying bad manners such as eating your lunch during sessions, or not being offered a coffee. But more serious things can happen as well. For example, one party might be overtired or be having personal problems, one person might remind the other of someone they dislike, the supervisor might be behaving in a superior or a suspicious way (and so might you as a supervisee, of course), or the training institute/employer might suddenly impose certain requirements on supervision that neither party is able to handle. In cases like these, it is vital to share your feelings and frustrations and to discuss them maturely; as always, supervision depends crucially on clear, open, and honest communication.

A truly capable supervisee (and supervisor!) is able to reflect on these things, to forgive them initially, and to bring them up for discussion again in a more reflective, exploratory manner. And in the event of any disruptions in the relationship, it is good for you as a supervisee to entertain the possibility that your own defences are at fault; perhaps you were simply over-sensitive because the stakes are so high for you in supervision and the process makes you feel exceptionally vulnerable. For example, feedback is often taken all too seriously, as a form of rejection or criticism, and that is when the sparks really start to fly in supervision. Moreover, due to the conversational nature of supervision, the process can stir up certain negative experiences from the past. For example, it can remind you of how you were always criticised during your music lessons, or how your parents only paid you any attention if you had under-performed in some way, and then only to tell you off, often failing to communicate to you the love and genuine care behind their concern. Supervision often feels like a reiteration of very early helping relationships, such as those with your parents, grandparents, or teachers. And if something went wrong back then in terms of personal feedback, it is not so perplexing that it should happen again in supervision.

The only advice we can give in this context is to stay tolerant of the relationship, to try to give it another chance, to accept your supervisor as a person—including all the potential harshness, vagueness or aloofness—and try to talk about the effects that this relationship is having on you and how hurt or misunderstood you sometimes feel during supervision. Always try to search actively for the "core of truth" in any harsh words or gestures from your supervisor, so you can at least derive the maximum learning benefit from them. And if you truly believe that your supervisor is still not responding positively to your good will and attempts at reconciliation, change supervisor and try again in a new supervision relationship. Changing supervisor will not always be easy, but it helps if you have discussed the tensions with your supervisor and can show that you have made attempts to improve your current supervisory relationship.

Case example

A clinical training programme involves lectures, training workshops, clinical seminars, and supervision groups of three. All of these programme elements start from the first week; however, at that stage the trainees are not yet seeing patients, so initially they have little to talk about at supervision. Instead of talking about this problem, the supervisor decides that "we'll have some fun going over some of the theoretical underpinnings in coming weeks; let's each read an article, take it in turns, and then we will talk about the article". Although the suggestion of such a reading group provided a solution to the problem, the three students had different expectations and wanted to hear something about practice: how to get patients in the first place, how to conduct oneself in first conversations with patients, etc. They talk with each other and reinforce their negative impressions of the start of this work, saying, "this is not supervision", "we are just being asked to keep ourselves busy talking about articles", and so on. This negative start continues to influence the two years of weekly supervision sessions. The group never gels. Facts about the group and the collaboration in the supervision combination are not being discussed. The students keep talking with each other about "pretending to be supervised", and generally both the feedback from the students and the reports from the supervisor become rather cold, if not outright negative. In retrospect it would have been better to tackle some of the problems in the group head on, and as early as possible.

3 Learning in supervision

Supervisors normally work with one to four supervisees at the same time, sometimes up to eight.[1] Supervision with one supervisee is described as *individual* supervision. After that, it becomes *triadic* supervision (two supervisees paired with one supervisor) or *group supervision*.

The size of the supervision combination can be determined by the sponsor. This decision can be made on didactic grounds (people learn differently in a group setting as compared with individually), but it can also be purely pragmatic (group supervision is cheaper per supervisee than individual supervision). The same usually applies to the length of the supervision period (number of sessions).

In professions where practitioners work primarily with groups, teams, families or classes, there is certainly something to be said for organising supervision at least partly in groups, as there is a strong possibility that the same patterns that supervisees struggle with in practice will also be played out in one way or another within a supervision group. If supervisees can learn to relate differently to the supervision group, it will also become easier for them to relate differently with groups of clients, pupils, or customers.

In defining supervision, we should consider the question, *"What does supervision mean to whom?"*

- For trainers and supervisors, supervision is a didactic method that can be used to achieve certain training or educational goals in a specific manner within a practical or professional training context.
- For students and trainees, supervision is a tailored learning opportunity that can benefit their professional practice. Within the overall supervisory framework, they can formulate their own learning issues and learning objectives.
- For service managers and care coordinators, supervision is a way to give staff a chance to improve their professional competence.
- For customers, clients and sponsors, supervision is an additional guarantee that the helping relationship is being conducted professionally.

3.1 How do people learn in supervision?

If the aim is to learn how to utilise insights for the benefit of professional action (see section 1.3), the key words are insight, learning, and action. While these certainly belong together in supervision, we can also consider each of these three aspects individually for a better understanding of what they involve.

Insight

The Concise Oxford English Dictionary describes insight as "the capacity to gain an accurate and deep understanding of someone or something". This understanding should not be interpreted as purely rational. The mind encompasses more than just the intellect: it also includes intuition, feelings, motives, desires, suspicions, opinions, and preconceptions. Insight, understood as the result of our thoughts, feelings and actions, can be acquired and developed by *reflecting*. This means looking back, contemplating, and searching for the meaning of what you have seen, experienced, thought, or done. In supervision, this practice of reflection aims to acquire insight that can lead to new or (more) conscious action in practice.

Learning

Learning in supervision is based on reflecting, inspired by questions such as: precisely what happened? How did it go? What does this mean for you and for others involved? Could you look at it differently? In what way, and how would that affect what happens next? How would you go forward from here? How will you do that, and what aids will you need? It may also help to take a look at the example in section 3.2.

It will become apparent that supervision is a form of experiential learning: learning from concrete practical experiences by reflecting on them and drawing conclusions. Your "learning material" or "case work" is supplied not by the supervisor but by yourself—based on your own experience in helping relationships or even more broadly in your career and life. Learning in supervision brings the following three aspects of that learning material together:

- *experiences* that you bring to supervision; note that experiencing means assigning meaning to the things that happen to you;
- making these experiences more *explicit* which entails placing them outside of yourself and looking at them as if from the outside;
- and then *reviewing* those experiences in a broader context, which means revisiting them (literally, to reflect or bend back those experiences in your mind) while assigning new meaning to the experience based on a different perspective, fresh state of mind, or new information.

Working thus on experience together with your supervisor, you can learn new professional action, which will lead in turn to new experience and in some cases to new reflection, and so on. Learning may take the form of a spiral that starts with becoming aware of and making contact with your experiences. At the outset, it can be difficult to see a practical experience as a personal one as well, and to figure out the connections between yourself and your experiences.

For example, how did you feel when a well-intentioned act on your part was misunderstood and met with an irritated response from those involved? Different people will attribute their own meaning to their experiences (i.e., their own interpretation of what happened), even if they experienced the exact same event with you.

Supervision gives you the opportunity in a safe space to explore what may have gone wrong in a given situation: you recount your experience (and by putting it into words you make it more explicit for yourself). Your supervisor listens and asks questions, helping you to see the experience through different eyes (and so helps you to "bend back" the experience and find new perspectives). You discover that the experience can also be interpreted differently; for example, a success can always also be viewed as a failure and vice versa. You decide on a new course of action. This leads in turn to new experiences, reflection, and so on.

Action

The experiences relevant to supervision therefore stem from your practice and the actions you undertake in practice. Supervision is mainly about you as a professional, you as a person doing the things that you do, professionally.

Acting professionally means doing what you do as part of your profession in a responsible, methodological manner. Acting professionally entails:

1. Acting *with awareness*, that is, having an understanding of what it is you are doing and why.
2. Acting *purposefully*, that is, with an idea in mind of what you want to achieve in this situation.
3. Acting *systematically*, that is, as much as possible guided by a structured approach or overarching philosophy.
4. Acting *procedurally*, that is, aided by sub-goals and a phased plan.

No doubt you have already learned about professionalism and professional actions at length in your training. Theory and practice seminars furthered by reading are the primary vehicles for teaching trainees what they need to do in their intended profession, and where its boundaries lie. Supervision builds on this. Supervision can teach you what this means for you in specific situations, and how to find or rediscover your own path and a personalised ideology as well as methodology. Initially, this is done with the aid of the experiences from your own practice that you bring into supervision. In parallel to that the process also draws on your behaviour during supervision itself, as a second source and opportunity for learning from experiences.

3.2 What should be learned in supervision?

Supervision was previously described (see Chapter 1) as an important form of learning for person- or client-centred jobs and helping professions. The supervisee will need to learn how to maintain a functional *relationship* and to handle *interactions* efficiently (for an explanation of these terms, see the Introduction). This includes the relationship and interactions that are needed between the practitioner and the person(s) with whom they are working for a particular period. Communication and relational skills are at the basis of professional practice, so acquiring these skills is a central task—in supervision as well.

However, an additional complication can arise with young practitioners who are just starting out on their career; you might want to consider the extent to which this applies to you. Section 1.3 mentioned potential problems that may be encountered when developing a professional identity at a time when your personal identity is still emerging. Students in higher professional education undertaking work placements sometimes have an awful lot to deal with at once. For example, they may also be undergoing changes in their personal relationships and circumstances (finding lodgings? moving house? a new relationship?). Supervision quickly becomes a central point where you can "finally get a chance to talk" and exchange experiences with peers. The supervisor does take account of this but will keep the focus on how to learn from such a variety of experiences in order to improve your professional competence.

In supervision, people should learn how to take their cues from practice and how to work together to further professional practice. To this end, a supervision combination together with one or more other supervisees can prove very useful!

Supervision is also about teaching supervisees to learn *independently* from practical experiences so that they can continue their own learning processes after the end of the supervision period. To encourage this independent learning, the following skills are especially important.

Reflecting

Learning from (work) experiences is a skill that can be developed. Where supervision is used to help supervisees practise their profession independently, reflecting on concrete work experiences is not the only tool available, but it *is* the most important one. Reflecting therefore has to be learned; the intention being that the supervisee can continue the art of reflecting independently once the supervision period is over. What does this require?

Making explicit

In order to learn effectively by reflecting on (work) experiences, those experiences will first have to be made concrete or explicit. This means making contact with what you have experienced, and retrieving the experience as specifically as possible. For example, if a supervisee complains about "grumpy patients on my ward", the supervisor can ask them to explain the problem more precisely.

Then it might turn out that Mrs A asked for a glass of water three times within the space of ten minutes. But the supervisee did not hurry to help and indeed had got angry because: "I'm already so busy and I can't stand her moaning."

Problematising

After making the experience explicit, you look for clues or leads in order to learn something from the situation. This process is called problematising, although it is not always necessarily about problems: a successful experience can be "problematised" as well. It is about analysing the experience, finding key components and identifying core issues and potentially your own personal points for improvement. To stay with our previous example, what exactly was the situation with Mrs. A? What did this mean for her and how did it make her feel? Why did the supervisee get angry? How did he experience the situation? Could he have seen it differently and, as a result, perhaps have responded differently to her request? How? Why did he not do that? Which aspects of his ward experience play into this?

Generalising

Once the situation itself has been explored and problematised, the supervisee can be invited to ask herself if the way she reacted is an isolated case or a regular occurrence. The opposite of making an experience concrete and specific is "generalising": exploring the extent to which certain behaviours or attitudes share general traits and might have to be identified as areas for development. The supervisee in our example might discover that he lacks patience in general for people who "moan", because moaning was discouraged by his parents in his youth. He therefore (unconsciously) attributes the cause of his own irritation to other people.

Finding learning objectives

Analysing an experience like this can reveal a need for supervisees wishing to learn from a practical experience to apply themselves to particular learning aims. For the supervisee in the example, the clash with Mrs A might raise questions about his own impatience when facing queries or requests from others ("moaning") and how he could change it. The supervisee could then address this theme or "learning issue" actively. In other words, he can begin to look for alternatives to this attitude and the resulting behaviour.

Evaluating

Finally, supervision also entails evaluating the outcome of learning. Evaluating means expressing a value judgement: what do you think of ...—and why? It is important that the context and aim of the evaluation are clear to those involved. It can also be useful to formulate a list of questions or points for attention in advance. Supervisor and supervisee can then consider how the outcome can be used to further the process.

Of course, the supervision itself will also be evaluated on several occasions. The focus here is both on what was achieved and on how that result was arrived at (*outcome* and *process*, respectively). A supervision evaluation is not complete unless and until questions have been considered such as: what have I still to learn in addition to what I have already achieved? And: how do I go about that?

3.3 Learning material in supervision

The sources of learning material are:

- The supervisee herself: who am I? What do I want? What do I do? How do I work? What are my strengths and weaknesses?
- The supervisee's professional practice: what do I come up against there? What does that mean for me? How can I relate to it? How do I want to relate to it?
- Professional training and standards: what do I need to learn to do this work? What are emerging issues in our practice? How is regulation evolving? What can we learn from research about practice?

These sources can also be seen as areas from which learning issues, tasks, or objectives can be derived in order to be processed in supervision. Often, in order to get them ready for processing, they first need to be put into words or made explicit. This can be done either verbally or in writing, preferably both. Your learning process benefits greatly if you can put things into specific terms. It often helps to apply some structure as well. Ideally you, your supervisor and your co-supervisees prepare thoroughly for every session.

Reporting

A useful tool to prepare for supervision is to have the supervisee(s) write reports or transcripts which then serve as a starting point for the conversation. Work experiences can be converted into learning experiences in the supervision session. Supervision material normally consists of written and verbal contributions from the supervisee, possibly supplemented by other aids (such as audio or video recordings, diagrams, drawings or other forms of expression). The written part may be sent to the supervisor and co-supervisees in advance. There are three types of report:

a. The reflection report
The supervisee is encouraged to commit a short review to paper after each supervision session. In this review, the supervisee describes what mattered or appealed to her most in the session, followed by an account of what this means to her, and the conclusions drawn or questions raised. At the next session, supervisee and supervisor take a look back at the session using this review and, if necessary, examine it in more depth.

b. The work contribution
The work contribution is also meant as a form of preparation for the next meeting. The supervisee chooses a practice experience, gives a description of it, and adds her own comments or questions for the supervisor. If the description is written up soon after the experience, it can record both the specific interventions used by the supervisee and the sense that the supervisee attributed to the meeting or conversation. Some supervisors prefer to have a description only of "observables", that is, specific interactions and words spoken between the supervisee and her clients or counterparts (which could be prepared from memory or as a literal "verbatim" transcript from a recording). The work contribution can also be read in advance of the supervision session.

As an alternative (or in addition) to a written work contribution, there is the option of using an audio or video recording relating to the work problem concerned. This should be done selectively, because listening to and viewing recordings can sometimes take up a lot of supervision time and might distract from the personal learning journey of the supervisee.

Here is a list of advantages and points to consider when comparing a "live" and a "non-live" work contribution in the form of either a ("live") report or a ("non-live") recording (see Wiggins, Bird, Reilly, Atter, & De Haan, 2014):

Advantages of a "live" contribution	Advantages of a (written) "reported" contribution	Advantages of a "recorded" (audio or video) contribution	Points to consider when using audio and video recordings
This is an informal, narrative process that can often quickly get to the heart of the issue.	The best of both worlds: reliable information about the case history, information about its processing, and a spontaneous presentation here and now.	Positive impact on the supervisory relationship: supervisee and supervisor listen to the material together, so the supervisee experiences less of a power imbalance.	Always seek your clients' permission before making a recording: they will usually see it as a sign of professionalism and will generally agree.
You can often learn more from your own "free associations" and behaviour here and now, than from the actual case history being related.	The "free associations"—from which so much can be learned—start with the way in which the report has been written.	Supervisee and supervisor can spot significant patterns in the supervisee's approach, patterns that generally remain largely invisible during other forms of supervision.	Tell clients in advance that you will use the recording only in supervision (and only once), and that you will then erase it to guarantee confidentiality.

(Continued)

(*Continued*)

In this form of supervision, participants in a "helping conversation" look at other "helping conversations" that often have a lot in common—experienced supervisors can often make good use of the resulting *parallel processes*.	Reporting on the supervision itself is simpler, because the supervisee can add to the written work contribution.	Helping professions are often solitary professions, which makes it unusual for a colleague to listen in on a helping conversation. An audio or video recording provides that opportunity: in a sense, the supervisor is looking over the supervisee's shoulder.	Record a variety of conversations in this way so that you have a selection to choose from for supervision. A mobile phone generally makes a good-enough recording device for supervisory purposes.
In this approach, you are least tied to the "original" material or "historical" fact—together with your supervisor, you can jump from one to the other and thus link to other aspects of your work.	This is an ideal method for exploring the often-defensive influences of memory and of reporting style. You learn to look at aspects of your work that you conveniently "forget".	Supervision based on an audio recording is a fairly slow process as it involves listening to isolated fragments. However, the resulting delay can enhance the reflective capabilities of both supervisee and supervisor.	Be open, and choose fragments that you have real doubts about. Bring those ones into supervision, even if it makes you anxious. A degree of tension and anticipation in your body is good for supervision, provided you trust your supervisor.

(*Continued*)

(*Continued*)

The "truth" of supervision exists mainly here and now.	The "truth" of supervision can be followed from (a) what happened, via (b) the initial processing in the report, to (c) the conversation here and now.	The "truth" of supervision exists there and then: sometimes refreshingly genuine and specific, and remains confined initially to the selection of the recording.	Consider sending the recording in advance, but only of course if your supervisor is open to this. It does save a lot of supervisory time if your supervisor has already heard or seen the recording.

c. Evaluation reports

Around halfway through the supervision period it is time to step back for a moment. One session is reserved for a *midterm evaluation* of the supervision process. This evaluation meeting is about the supervisee's learning effects and learning process to date, and about the situation and the working relationship in supervision. It also looks at the extent to which objectives, agreements, and methods need to be adjusted (although this can also be done in the interim if required). As a form of preparation and a basis for the conversation, the supervisee can write an evaluation report that is then studied by the supervisor. In training supervision, this can be followed by a final or provisional assessment by the supervisor. Points to think about for the following period are then agreed upon.

At the end of the supervision period, it is time for a *final evaluation*. Both the preparation and the discussion are very similar to those in the midway evaluation. The difference is that, instead of making any adjustments needed, the participants round off the supervisory process and say goodbye. In training supervision, the results achieved are also assessed. This is often a combination of self-assessment by the supervisee and the supervisor's final views; the latter are important for the purpose of qualification.

NB: the evaluation process will reveal that the reflection reports are a useful aid in identifying the connecting themes that run through your learning process; and your supervisor may refer to those themes again at the end.

Case example

An experienced clinician retrains for working with couples and as part of his training he has to do 150 hours of "supervised practice", which in the last two years of his qualification means seeing one couple longer term and having one individual supervision session every two weeks on this work with them. The supervision is based on transcripts of sessions that the supervisee prepares for every supervisory meeting. In the final midterm review the supervisor writes among other positive feedback and "satisfactory" assessments, "Trainee is an established professional, so not always amenable to suggestions. For example, I suggested he clarify whether he could extend the period of therapy before discussing it with the couple, but he felt confident that he had this leeway." And later, "Comes prepared to supervision, but though he responds positively, my impression is that he is somewhat 'formed' as a therapist and therefore less able to take on board a slightly different way of thinking. I have not seen much evidence of the trainee assimilating discussions that have taken place in supervision."

This review led to a conversation between the clinician and his course director, as was usual on that programme. When the feedback above was raised the course leader asked for the trainee's view, which was balanced between "maybe I could be more open to suggestions" and "this supervisor does not seem to insist on a lot of guidance". At that point the course leader said "Don't you think it is *very serious* if you come across as a fully formed practitioner who is not open to suggestions from your supervisor? Just imagine what that might mean for how you work with your patients—with such a closed frame of mind! You want soon to become qualified as a relationship therapist and for us to approve how you work; this will be quite difficult for us if you are not open to your supervisor's suggestions."

At this point the conversation between them became hard and even bitter, and the clinician only learned over time that indeed he had been more resistant to guidance than he thought. Ultimately, he had to work very hard in the last term of his study to demonstrate his supervisor's influence on his practice. To his relief it said on the final evaluation sheet: "The trainee took on board the comments made in the previous supervision report and has tried to be more receptive to discussions that have taken place in supervision."

4 Reflective assignment

To get a feel for the material in previous chapters and to make it relevant, we propose a personal assignment: a two-part reflection exercise relating to your experience of supervision.

Imagine you are going on a trip to "supervision land" say in a month's time, and that you already have some idea of what might await you there. You already know your fellow travellers/co-supervisees, but not your guide/supervisor, apart from their name and email address. The supervisor has apparently asked each supervisee to submit a written presentation in advance, and you have decided to take up the challenge. You are therefore going to write a letter to your supervisor about what would be best for you.

First focus on the kind of person you are

For supervisees who have not undertaken any supervision before, it can be useful to prepare for the first encounter with your supervisor by thinking about certain aspects of your life, especially how and why you became the person you are today. To help with this, you could write a letter to yourself, based on questions such as the following:

- What was the family or community into which you were born and in which you grew up? What was your social context and that of your family?
- Who were important people in that environment? What were the prevailing views, convictions, values, norms, rules of behaviour?
- What sort of primary and secondary education did you receive? What were your preferences and achievements in education? How did you spend your free time?
- What led you to choose this profession or training? What attracts you to it most?
- To what extent is your choice of profession related to your life history, family background, education, etc.?
- How would you like to live and work, now and in the future—what is your ideal in, say, twenty years' time? What would you like this profession to bring you personally?

Now write the letter to your supervisor about what you want to achieve by participating in supervision, and include at least the following:

- Say what your practice is all about, who your clients are, and how it is going.
- Say something about your experience in your profession or professional training. Try to mention a few highlights and regrets along the way.
- If you have already formed a view on this, try to say where your strengths/weaknesses lie with respect to your work in helping relationships.
- Share what you expect or hope to gain from supervision, from your supervisor and your co-supervisees, and what they can expect from you.
- Work out a number of (provisional) learning goals and desirable outcomes.
- Write about something else that matters to you, something that might say more about you than all of the above.

If you have written these letters, keep them. This type of self-reflection translated into words can also be of excellent service later on, for example, when you review supervision to see if it has achieved its aims for you.

Case example
After completing her studies in economics and organisational science, Louise finds her first job as a researcher in a consultancy firm. Over the first four years she demonstrates that not only is she a very conscientious researcher but also she is good with clients and can be trusted to explain and present statistical results directly in front of clients. Then she is promoted to junior consultant and for her own development is offered a four-day workshop on Consulting Skills. This helps her to be less defensive with clients and to ask more questions and listen better; however, she feels nowhere near professional in the mature helping conversations that are now her daily remit.   At this point she decides to contract with one of the clinical psychologists from the course, to have regular conversations about her practice and work. After a first run of eight sessions they decide on six sessions a year, a contract which remains in place for the next eight years until Louise makes a change to another consultancy. Louise only finds out much later that the work she did with the psychologist is in fact called supervision. She would argue that she was mainly acquiring more consulting skills, as well as making sense of the feedback she received on the job (mostly from more senior colleagues rather than from her clients who were generally positive). She would add that the regular conversations with her supervisor also helped her steer her own path through the organisational politics of her consultancy.

Part II

Being on the supervisory journey

*Your supervisory process, including common
themes in supervision*

The decision has been taken: you are going on a trip to a largely
unknown faraway land. It will be a journey of discovery into almost
virgin territory. You are already aware of the opportunities that the
journey holds and the conditions under which you can set off. You now
know your fellow travellers and your guide, but you have not yet met
up to talk about the journey itself. You could say that the preliminary
phase is complete. Now the formalities have been taken care of, the
supervision can begin.

Part II is intended for *new supervisees* and is about the different stages
of the supervision process: the initial, middle, and final stage. A *process* is a staged evolution, "a series of actions or steps taken in order to
achieve a particular end" (Concise Oxford English Dictionary). Like the
previous part of the book, this part rounds off with an exercise and a
worked example. Part III then goes on to look at certain philosophical
aspects in more depth. ✓

5 The initial stage

As soon as supervisor and supervisee(s) have met for the first time, the supervision can begin. Quite naturally, the initial activities include getting to know each other and starting the supervisory relationship. At the same time, the participants begin to share and compare their wishes, expectations, and aims. This is also when they start to create conditions and agree ground rules: the supervisory contracting (see section 2.2) has begun.

The most important aspect of the initial stage is a joint (and mostly implicit) exploration of how to create an effective climate for learning, a learning situation that is both safe and challenging, both confidential and reliable. This is especially crucial in training supervision, on account of its compulsory nature: placement(s) and supervision are part and parcel of the training. Important questions are: how does the supervisee perceive this compulsory nature of the relationship, and can the supervisee trust the relationship? Does the supervisee already know the supervisor and/or co-supervisees from a different context? Do the co-supervisees already know each other? How can any emerging doubts, sensitivities, or difficulties be made explicit and overcome?

Other aspects of the initial stage include drawing up an overall programme and making a start on the supervision. The initial stage covers the first one to three sessions and then concludes with a (provisional) working plan in the shape of the supervision contract (for a pro-forma model of a contract, see Appendix A). In this plan, each supervisee identifies a number of learning issues or challenges to consider for themselves and their own practice. These are then incorporated into the supervision contract as personal learning objectives.

5.1 Who are you both and how can you relate to each other?

The relationship between the participants in supervision can be described as a functional working relationship. This means that the interactions between the partners are determined by the goal they are setting out to achieve. Supervisor and supervisee(s) each have their own role, tasks, and responsibilities within the relationship.

Functional relationship

Functional relationships can be based on *symmetry*: for example, where members of a study or work group come together for this sole purpose on a basis of reciprocity. Such relationships can also be founded on *asymmetry*: a teacher sets out to impart the course's content to her students, while the converse does not apply.

Supervision relationships belong to the latter group: the supervisor is focused on the supervisee's learning. To achieve supervision goals, however, a good *working relationship* is required between supervisor and supervisee. They are equal partners in that relationship. At the same time all other aspects that are relevant to relationships are bound to be relevant here (see also the Introduction of this book): supervision is an ongoing process of communicative interaction between people, involving an exchange of personal experiences, perceptions, feelings and expectations. In sum, we can discern within the supervisory relationship a hierarchical relationship (where the supervisor may have power over the supervisee and the client may have a different power over the supervisor), a working relationship with a common aim, and an ordinary relationship full of perceptions and expectations.

Functional relationships are terminated when the final goal has been attained or is deemed unattainable, when the work comes to an end, or when the specified or agreed time period has elapsed. This does not necessarily mean that the connection or rapport is broken, because other types of relationship (functional or otherwise) may also exist, develop or be continued between the participants, which is normally fine.[1]

Getting to know each other

People embarking on a supervisory relationship would do well to start by getting to know each other better. By doing so, you give each other some understanding of who you are, where/how/ with whom you live, work, and study, and how you experience these things.

For the purposes of supervision, it is also relevant to know how the other person perceives their profession, what their job entails, how motivated they are to do it, what they want to achieve in it and with it, or what they hope or expect to gain through their work. It is relevant at the start to find out whether and to what extent you as supervisee are already familiar with supervision. Some supervisees will have had supervision before; for others, it may be their first time. What sort of experiences have they had in the past, and what impressions does the supervisee have now of the supervision and supervisor?

As part of this getting-to-know-you process, *information can be exchanged on two levels*: in terms of content and in terms of perception or relationship (see Watzlawick, Beavin, & Jackson, 1967). Greatly simplified, these levels can be described as follows (this is also useful to remember for other situations, for example, in your own professional practice):

- The *content level*: what is the message that you want to get across, the content of the information? You can exchange information such as: what do I know, what do I want, what can I do (what can I not do yet), and what are my reasons for coming here?
- The *relationship level*: how should the content be understood, what does the information mean? Supervision is also about "tuning in" to each other: who am I, who are you, what are we doing, how do we live, how do we make sense of our lives and ourselves, how do we experience our profession and studies, how are we motivated?

Note that as a general rule, the better people know each other, the faster they understand each other's intentions. Close friends, for example, sometimes "only need to say a word" for both parties to know where they stand and what they want. On the other hand, in functional relationships it is important to "play it safe" and not be too quick to assume that you fully understand the other person. Given the sensitivity of supervision it is essential to keep accepting, inquiring into and appreciating the other person as a different and valuable person, and not to dismiss out of hand when there are difficulties (see also Chapter 2 about difficulties in the supervisory relationship).

Boundaries

It is important to keep an eye on the boundaries, both in the supervisory relationship and in the getting-to-know-you process that starts the supervision off. Boundaries are defined by respect for each other and the objective of supervision: personal learning to further your professional practice.

As soon as it becomes harder to retain the combination of mutual respect and a shared objective, then personal boundaries may be violated and you may find the other person intrusive, or withholding, or unprofessional. For supervision to run smoothly, therefore, both supervisees and supervisor will need to take care to remain respectful and aware of the mutually shared objective, so as to avoid any unwilling and undesirable, even accidental, crossings of personal boundaries.

Each party has the right to call a halt if the focus on the person is becoming too intense for them. But equally, it is not good if the focus on the practical aspects of the work becomes so strong that the *person* of the worker disappears from view. Supervision entails a delicate balance between content and relationship, between "professional" feedback and "personal" feedback, and requires supervisor and supervisee to be in broad agreement on this balance.

5.2 Who are you both and what can you do together?

Apart from exploring individual aspects as they get to know each other, the partners should also look at the supervision combination itself. How did this particular matching of supervisor and supervisee come about? What does it mean for their working relationship? As a general rule, the possible scenarios are as follows:

- The supervision partners (supervisor and supervisee or supervisees) already knew each other (to some extent), or they did not know each other at all.
- The supervision partners were able to choose each other, or they had little or no influence on the composition of the supervision combination.

In group supervision, supervisees may already know each other and may have had a say in the group's composition, but this does not usually apply with regard to the supervisor. In training supervision, the practice is often to appoint a supervisor (who may be unknown to the students). In supervision in other contexts and for more mature professionals, the freedom of choice is normally greater.

Complications

In supervision groups where supervisees have chosen each other, it is important to be on the alert for potential complications. It can benefit the supervision to establish why the participants are so keen to go into supervision with a particular person, in the earliest stages of the process. What do you expect from each other? What do you think you can learn from the other person? Why do you want to go into supervision with your best friend?

If supervision partners like each other and even have strong feelings for each other, this can also put a block on learning in supervision. They are able and willing to support each other but often lack the nerve to ask each other controversial questions. However, for everyone's learning process to run smoothly in group supervision, it is vital not only for the supervisor to "work" but also for co-supervisees to support each other *and* to ask difficult questions. Problems can be avoided if the participants bear this in mind and are not too wedded to their "friendships" in the supervision group. The supervisor can help you in saying something challenging to your buddy, with encouragement, safety, and reliability.

Aligning expectations

In supervision situations, the supervisor tries to be clear from the outset on what the supervisee expects from the supervisor. Vice versa it is also important to understand what the supervisor is expecting and what the co-supervisees expect from each other. The supervisor can then help to establish a realistic rapport and possibly to adjust wishes and expectations, against the background of the objective of supervision in your specific context.

This process of aligning relationships and content can lead to the conclusion: yes, we like the look of this, we do want to go on this journey of discovery together! In the majority of cases, this is what happens. But if the process is bumpy or brings major differences to light, there will need to be further discussions: within the group and possibly with the sponsor of supervision as well. The outcome of these discussions might prompt a change in the supervision combination (see also Chapter 2).

5.3 What can you achieve and how?

If the above has led to a positive outcome, it is time for a specific working agreement or plan. The content of this plan depends on the answers to the following questions (see also sections 3.2 and 5.1):

a. Which phase of which professional training course is the supervisee in at present? To what extent does the training programme contain profession- and practice-oriented aspects that the supervision can build on?
b. How much and what type of practical experience does the supervisee already have? In which profession and which post? Where is the supervisee working during the supervision period? Which duties does it entail?
c. What does the supervisee still want and need to learn? How does the supervisee normally learn best?

Learning objectives

The working agreement for supervision includes plans on the part of the supervisee(s). These plans are devised on the basis of what the supervisee already knows and can already do, and they contain specific items for (the first part of) the supervision period. Some examples are:

• A supervisee in higher professional education in the field of nursing finds that she loses her patience quickly with certain patients. In her plan she says: "I want to find out exactly why that happens, and how I can change it. What is it exactly that makes me impatient with one person and not with another? What do I find so hard to cope with, that I often end up being short with people? I don't like it, but how can I change it? I want to use the supervision to figure this out and improve. In order to work on this in my work contribution I will cite practical situations in which this has happened. I am keen to hear your reactions and am hoping for your help so that I can start to do it differently."

- A novice teacher could include the following in his supervision plan: "How can I learn to tune in better to what is going on in the class?" Or: "How can I learn to handle my anxiety in class?" Or: "How can I overcome my fear of that particular group of pupils?"
- A social worker just starting out in the profession might want to use supervision to learn how to handle aggressive youths, the elderly or people with dementia. But there could also be a different type of problem: "In my institution I am often asked for help by people whose level of education is higher than mine. I have to work with them to find a solution, but how can I overcome my own insecurity and feel less intimidated?"
- A trainee art therapist might already be highly skilled in her medium (music, drama, visual art) but, in her placement in a school for children with learning difficulties, she doesn't know how to make contact with the pupils and to actually do something for them. In supervision, she wants to learn how to function effectively in her practice.

A provisional learning programme is best committed to paper; it forms part of the material submitted for supervision. Devising and writing down plans is a useful aid but, of course, it should not lead to rigidity. A plan for supervision should be flexible and changeable if the need arises or if the situation demands it. For example, a learning aim may be achieved and become outdated, or it may need to be amended in the course of time.

Methods

The general working material for supervision includes the learning and working plans ("professional development plans") and their content, as well as considerations about the forms these plans might take. A regular feature is usually written reflection, as are current work contributions for the supervision sessions (see section 3.3). For working through all of these, the methods to be used need to be broadly agreed.

A range of tools can be used to process the learning material, in addition to simply talking about it. Examples include audio recordings, role-play, communication exercises, and non-verbal techniques (posture, mimicry, movement, modelling, drawing, music, group constellations, etc.). Choices in this regard depend partly on the methods and options available to the supervisor, but can also be based on how supervisees learn best from their own experiences. Some supervisees want to "see" first before they "know", and some vice versa. Others need concrete and practical options to go on first, before they have the nerve to contemplate or undertake the next step. Some learn from the abstract to the concrete, and the opposite can be true for others.

Think about how this applies to you: which learning and working style have you developed? Think back on one of the greatest inspirations for learning in your life, a time when you experienced accelerated learning and development. Then make a list for yourself of the key ingredients of that exceptional learning for you. Try to find the "active ingredients" in that learning: was it the environment, was it pressure or actually lack of pressure, was it a particular teacher or guide, or was it something particularly enjoyable or something you knew you could go on to achieve with the learning?

Each person, each supervisee, has her own way of going about things. In supervision, you can put this to good use in using best strategies from the past and also finding your own path for learning in this profession.

In addition, one supervision combination can be more creative than another, especially where it comes to spotting and exploiting parallels between current supervision methodology and practice. However, differences in learning and working style can also lead to tension within the supervision combination (see also our comments in section 2.3). These will have to be resolved in the supervision relationship itself; after all, supervisees will need to (learn how to) handle differences between themselves and clients, patients or partners in their professional practice as well.

Case example

Robin is extremely successful as a clinical psychologist. He has chosen his father's profession and quickly became a "golden boy" in the various places where he has worked. He has had a practice in his father's teaching hospital from age twenty-five and he is now the director of a large clinic, as well as taking time to see many of the more challenging patients.

At age thirty-eight he has decided to return to supervision. He first met his supervisor Alison when she held a lecture on supervision at a national NHS conference. It was as if he first needed to be convinced of her status in the field. At his first supervision session he arrives on time, not a minute early, not a minute late, and he is dressed in a sharp suit with a bright red tie, much more elegantly than his supervisor. From the first minute Robin shows his commitment by divulging all the main events in his childhood, his intense grief over losses, his loneliness at times, and periods of bullying at school. His account of how he already started private practice when he was still studying is impressive, and he seems to have a lot of insight in his own competitiveness and ambition. His relationship with his father has been tumultuous and painful, and in the end he feels he has overcome the difficulties by telling his father exactly when he can visit and for how long. Robin appears to have won all the battles in his life except for the ones with necessity where he has had to suffer major losses.

He and his supervisor look at this state of affairs and try to make sense of it. Robin speaks about the admiration he gets from female patients and Alison raises the sensitive topic of erotic transference. Although Robin says he was never directly challenged, he did have to interrupt sessions to "get a glass of water", in order to extract himself from the erotic spells. He also admits to feeling "awkward" in the moment as he is telling this to Alison. Alison informs him about the high incidence rates of boundary crossings in the therapeutic profession, and she advises him to read an article about the damage that such crossings can cause. At the end of the session she thanks him for his openness and asks him to keep bringing areas where he feels ashamed and implicated, even if it may sometimes feel very difficult to do so. They plan ahead for regular sessions, which should help him stay on the right side of ethical practice. Over the course of the next week Alison writes up a draft working agreement where she summarises the highly per-sonal themes in somewhat more abstract professional language, as a first "formulation" of Robin's request and needs.

6 The middle stage

As the saying goes, well begun is half done. If the initial stage of supervision has gone well, you have laid a vital foundation for what comes next and you can get down to work. The transition can be gradual and almost unnoticed, or you can mark it by listing your ground rules, preferably on paper. A written contract is recommended, especially for individual supervision (see Appendix A for a model contract).

The middle stage of supervision is where the actual work or implementation takes place, where the supervisee's learning process is broadened and deepened. This stage can be broken down into three parts: the preparation, start and period leading up to the midterm review; the midterm review itself; the period afterwards until the supervision is complete. Plans from the initial stage are put into action and tested against the reality of working and learning in combination with each other.

6.1 Work in progress

As indicated above (section 1.3), supervision aims to integrate the personal (thoughts, feelings, wishes) in order to benefit the supervisee's actions in independent professional practice in specific work situations.

Integration means incorporating parts into a coherent whole. Integration is a process of making whole, of making complete. In the context of supervision, it can mean creating space for new insights and experiences among old and familiar ones, giving rise to a new unified whole.

Integration at the level of the person

Integration at the first level means achieving coherence between thoughts, feelings, wishes, and actions. In other words: knowledge, feelings, attitude and skills are coordinated in such a way as to allow expert, professional action on the part of this person. This may seem straightforward, but in practice there often turns out to be something wrong with this coordination, that is, with the intended coherence between the parts. Some aspects receive a stronger or weaker emphasis than others, sometimes rightly, but sometimes not. See the following examples:

- Skilful *action* can be over-emphasised in posts that involve various degrees of nursing, care, and services; sometimes at the expense of critical thinking or empathy with the other person.
- *Aiming and achieving* can be over-stressed in legal or accounting professions where monitoring, compliance or defence of values, or standards of behaviour play a leading role.
- *Feeling or empathy* can be dominant in social, therapeutic and pastoral practices. Thinking can sometimes seem less important.
- *Thinking* can be greatly exaggerated in the post-session reflections of a professional practitioner. Without supervision this kind of thinking may well become circular and take the form of rumination or "lazy thinking" when the practitioner relies on fixed convictions or on stale and ossified ideas from training or reading.

Integration at the level of the profession

Integration at the second level means that the above-mentioned coherence between thoughts, feelings, and wishes in the person is strong enough to incorporate the practice of the profession, with everything that entails. The more successful this process, the greater the supervisee's professional competence. After all, professional expertise, or competence in a particular post, is a direct result of the ability to bring together theory and practice, strategy and skills, and intention and execution.

In this process, your professional practice benefits from:

- *General knowledge* that serves as a basis for your profession, particularly knowledge from the social, behavioural and organisational sciences.
- *Specific knowledge* about the profession: historical cases, basic principles, miscellaneous ideas and concepts.
- *Methodology* (ranging from approach to structure to procedure): basic principles and rules, general knowledge and ideology, improvisation and creativity.

"Practice" means the comprehensive, specific work situation in which the profession is pursued:

- *The organisation*: an institution, business or other occupational setting in which the work is carried out.
- *The clients* who receive or request the services provided.
- *The practitioners* and their roles, tasks and positions.
- *The philosophy* that underpins all of the above. This includes matters such as overall objectives and their interpretation, policies and implementation, views on methodology, professional qualifications, and so on.

Supervisees faced with the task of integrating within themselves person and profession, and on another level also theory and practice, can use supervision to figure out how to achieve integration. A major boost can come from the working relationship with the supervisor (i.e. within the supervision combination), driven by the relationship between the supervision partners and the resulting support.

The supervisory relationship

The asymmetric involvement of the participants (see sections 3.2 and 5.1) in a functional relationship can also serve to some extent as a model for various helping relationships that you as a supervisee have in your professional practice. However, there may be differences in terms of objectives. Whereas supervision is mainly about the supervisee's *learning*, other forms of direct or indirect services may be central to the supervisee's practice (direct services are focused on clients/patients/residents; indirect services are geared towards other professionals who in turn provide direct services).

Unlike ordinary personal relationships, which are a goal in themselves, functional relationships can be entered into and used as a means towards a separate goal. In order to use a relationship intentionally, you first need to raise awareness of the relationship, how it is forming, evolving, and why it came about. Then you can figure out what the "intentional use" means in this particular relationship.

A relationship or link between people is created through shared experience. It is founded on experiences in which people feel emotionally involved. The link is strengthened by the (verbal and non-verbal) exchange of thoughts and feelings about those experiences.

Relationships can be positively or negatively "tinged". This depends on the extent to which people agree with each other and/or have *sympathy* for each other, or indeed its opposite: *antipathy*. Both sympathy and antipathy strengthen the link.

Remember that, in many forms of service or care provision, the results achieved depend (in part) on the quality of the relationship, that is, the degree to which the worker is found to be sympathetic, knowledgeable and confidence-inspiring. Clients who dislike you are often not prepared to make full use of the services you offer, even if the services themselves are excellent. The same will be true in your relationship with your supervisor.

Working together

A good working relationship in supervision is not based on thin air; nor is it created simply by exchanging personal information. A supervisory relationship is forged by working together on the tasks that follow from the shared endeavour and have been agreed. In concrete terms, these tasks boil down to processing the learning material contributed by the supervisee, specifically their personal reflections and work contribution (section 3.3).

The practice experiences contributed, both in writing and verbally, are examined more closely under the direction of the supervisor and, increasingly, with the assistance of co-supervisees. The supervisee is invited to flesh out this (first) account in more detail:

- What are or were the facts, what exactly happened?
- What meaning do you assign to it yourself, and what is your opinion?
- What happened in the contact (at relationship level) between yourself and the other person(s)? (See section 5.1)
- What is your (provisional) conclusion, or what questions do you have for supervision?

The supervisee recounts their story, giving both himself and the listener(s) an understanding of what happened. Only once the supervisee has finished (and has been listened to attentively) is it time for questions such as: How can we look at this differently? What can be learned from this experience? (See also sections 3.1 and 3.2.)

The second account

It is important now to think carefully about the supervisee's story, their first account: the time for reflection has come. To develop a "second account", the supervisor will encourage you to take a fresh look at the experience, to review it with the help of questions such as:

- Could the facts have been interpreted differently, that is, other than my initial interpretation? For example, if more details had been given or in the light of what else I know about this client?
- How can a theoretical vision or methodological model, as discussed in training, help me in this regard?
- What insight emerges from my new perspective on the events?
- What conclusions do I draw, and what questions do I still have?
- How can I take this forward, and in what way could I handle it differently?

Once the supervisee's first story has been followed by a reflection or second account as described above, the supervisor can help you to look at what this particular (learning) experience means for your performance in other (similar) situations within your professional practice. What can you learn from this more generally? What might it tell us about you that you have presented this kind of work contribution and went away with this kind of resolve?

It is useful to remember that the supervisee's second account will not necessarily follow the first immediately. This can depend on a range of things, such as the complexity of the problem or the time available in this particular supervision session. Mostly it depends on the supervisee's need to process things quietly for a while before picking up where they left off. After all, everyone learns and reflects in their own unique way (section 5.3). Although the supervision dialogue often initiates and informs the process, much of the supervisee's reflections normally emerge in the interval between supervision sessions. This is when the actual work is done, when the practice is re-entered and the impetus for change and learning is largest. The supervisee then returns to this in the next session or later, posing new questions or explaining what they have learned from the previous experience and how those lessons have been put into practice.

6.2 The midterm review

In most cases, a supervision session is concluded with a short review in which the partners sum up their satisfaction with the session. For example:

- We worked really well today.
- I noticed that you—one supervisee in a group—didn't say very much for the last half hour; is something wrong?
- Once you—the supervisor—had commented that ..., I couldn't concentrate any more on what ... was saying.
- It bothered me that we skipped our coffee break, but I didn't want to make an issue of it.

Supervisees can also use their reflection report to review the session or give their views on (aspects of) its content, working relationships or methods used. This can all be examined again in the next session.

But the *midterm review* is a slightly unusual event. It is an instructive look back with a view to the future. Time can be set aside in the preceding supervision session to prepare for the midterm review, in terms of both content and form. The main topic of the review is the supervisee's learning process and the effects of supervision on performance in professional practice. The format of supervision, that is, the working relationship and methods used in the supervision combination, is also evaluated.

Evaluation report

Some supervisors expect their supervisee to write an evaluation report (see section 3.3). The starting points for this are the (learning) objectives, personal plans, and supervisory methods agreed during the contracting process (sections 2.2 and 5.3). If the training or qualifying institution has stipulated assessment criteria, these are included as well. In addition, your own earlier reflection reports are an excellent beginning for writing the evaluation report. The supervisor can also give some advice or pointers on how you might produce your report. For example:

- Consider the learning objectives, plans, and wishes you had on entering supervision.
- Have there been any changes or additions to these? Have your questions been (sufficiently) addressed? What remains outstanding?
- Have you noticed any effects of supervision on your way of working? What, where and how?
- How do you perceive our working relationship? What aspects of it promote or inhibit your learning? Would you like to see a change or shift in the relationship? Specifically, what?
- What do you want to work on in future, and how can supervision make a difference?
- Do you have anything else you wish to add?

Evaluation session

The supervisee's report forms the basis for the subsequent evaluation session. The supervisor and (in group supervision) the co-supervisees have reviewed the experience with you and read your report. When your turn comes, they will ask you questions, offer comments or try in other ways to supplement your own evaluation. The supervisor can round this evaluation off with a provisional opinion, having her or his own view on the results achieved, in light of the training, professional requirements and the objectives for supervision.

The session will then focus on the forthcoming supervision period. What still needs to happen before the final evaluation by the supervisor? To what extent will goals, plans, methods, and working alliances need to be adjusted? This can be seen as supplementary contracting, as a guideline for the supervision sessions to come. The supervisee includes the results of the evaluation session in their reflection report, ensuring that the midterm review can be completed in the following session.

At this mid-way point the supervisor also often produces a review report on how you have done in supervision, which you can discuss with the supervisor or as the case may be with your course or work manager, who may be receiving other reflections on how you have been doing as well. This will help you to see how the supervisor is independently evaluating the supervisory work. Some supervisors choose to show you the report before they share it with others, but that is not always the case. Reading a critical report can be painful and difficult and may require you to seek help from outside your supervisory combination. On the other hand, a critical report can also give you fresh ideas about your development. It may become an important impetus towards working on the themes mentioned by the supervisor. It is advisable to engage your supervisor in this "working through" of her or his tough feedback, and to enlist their support in improving your practice along the lines suggested (if only for "political" reasons: to enlist their support next time when evaluation comes along).

Obviously there can be more than one "midterm" review during the course of a supervisory journey, for example, termly or yearly on a qualifying course, or bi-yearly for experienced practitioners.

6.3 Heading towards the end

The midterm review is an important time in the supervision process, both for the individual supervisee and for the supervisee's relationship with the supervisor and co-supervisees. The achievements in the first stage have been considered, acknowledged, experienced, shared, and evaluated by the participants. This is a solid basis that can be built on in the final stage.

If the supervision so far has gone to plan, you are now able to learn more independently and to develop more personalised learning objectives. In group supervision, the process of "learning from each other" has also got off the ground. All of this means that the nature of the supervision will start to change and focus more on deepening the learning process than on exploring and broadening the scope of learning.

Reflecting and the importance of language

As you and your supervisor are trying to deepen reflection you will both become curious about the quality of your reflections, and about your own growing reflective skills (see section 3.1 and section 6.1, about the "second account"). Deepening your reflections is a very personal and often surprising experience, as you move from contemplating, to exchanging views, to considering alternatives, to trying to disentangle your feelings and your feelings from facts, to acknowledging your own defensiveness around certain sensitive areas, to seeking new connections within the material, and back to contemplation again as the case may be. It is not uncommon for a "light bulb" to come on suddenly: "Oh, that's how it all fits together! But then it could also be like this or like that! Why would I go on like this if I could do it differently, and probably better? I'm going to change my approach!" During supervision you as a supervisee build on your own reflection, in communication with supervisor and co-supervisees, with or without non-verbal methods.

Language is essential to supervision even if we make sense of our experience in many non-verbal ways, through images, feelings, dreams. Just like in most helping professions supervision uses language to convey what sense we are making, so in supervision you will reflect in large part aided by language, both spoken and written language.

There is a fundamental difference between speaking a language and writing in it:

- In *speaking*, ideas take shape in direct engagement with others. In order to stay connected and fluid, the conversational situation requires a degree of objective and logical thought. Moreover, through their verbal and non-verbal responses, interlocutors can help the speaker to express their thoughts more clearly.
- In *writing*, you have to rely on yourself to give shape to your ideas. The reader cannot access or examine them until a later stage. For the writer, therefore, it is vital to express their ideas in such a way that the reader understands what is meant. Compared with a spoken conversation, the partners in a written "conversation" have to meet higher standards in terms of their capacity for abstract and logical thought.

Writing

Clearly, it is vital to learn how to reflect on your casework in writing, as well as verbally. This can be a tough job for some practitioners, but the returns are huge. Committing your reflections to paper, that is, reflecting in writing, is above all a crucial tool which can help you learn to think better and more independently, for example, you practice putting your feelings into words and telling your story in an organised and coherent way. This provides you with a competence you can use to learn independent from supervision and in contracting with your clients.

Supervision can be a good place to overcome resistance to writing and a place where you can learn, without too much effort, how to do it better. As your reflective writing gains in quality, you will notice the supervision itself accelerating and you will be able to spend less time on clarifying your meaning. If you experience this sort of resistance to writing, it is a good idea to bring it up for discussion in your supervision. Then the supervisor can help you explore how to overcome the problem (see also the example described in section 8.2).

Case example

Over time in supervision one can get a real feeling of partnership and "comrades in adversity": a strong bonding with your supervisor and group. This can happen in individual and group supervision in equal measure, provided supervisees feel they can bring their professional concerns and challenges quite freely.

Here is an example from an open supervision group that has been offering regular supervision to a forty-strong community of practice for the last five years. Supervisees sign on for several sessions a year to keep a measure of quality control in their practice. On this day, long before the supervisor arrives, members of the group are trickling in, and they are enthusiastically updating each other on how they are, what recent transitions have happened in their lives, and they engage in some relaxed banter. They are helping each other to coffee and when formal supervision begins they are keen to give a short summary of their work and of particular recent clients before stating the issues they would like to be supervised on.

They use the rest of the morning to work on five different cases, facilitated by the supervisor. For some of those work contributions members of the group exercise their skills by doing twenty minutes of one-to-one work on them with the rest of the group watching. One of the participants, Ravinder, who has recently moved into a purely managerial role, uses the occasion to refresh her experience of conducting a helping conversation.

At the end Ravinder enjoys universal acclaim for how well she held her own in that short conversation and how in twenty minutes she really helped her peer supervisee to a few breakthroughs. In particular she receives praise for her courage in drawing attention to a moment where her (peer) supervisee looked away at the facilitator of the group, twice, and she wondered with her what may have happened in that moment.

Later, during the next short peer supervision session both partners seem to conclude that the client they speak about, who cried through large parts of sessions, is really not progressing during the work and should be referred to another form of help. At that point the supervisor feels he needs to step in. So in the group review afterwards he makes it clear that he thought the client might actually still be benefitting from the sessions with the supervisee, and might even be strongly attached to the work, and that in any case a "rejection" at this stage is a rather risky strategy and in his view not recommended. The group spends some time to think through why this idea of bringing the work to a close prematurely has arisen in the first place.

They also spend some time working on two other cases as a group of seven, by listening to the case and then taking turns in giving something back to the case bringer: a feeling, sensation or thought that has occurred to them as they listened to the case bringer bringing his challenge. At the end of the morning some in the group stay behind, to chat and exchange articles and confirm their hopes to re-join soon as it has been such a good session. The supervisor receives two emails afterwards from members of the group with thanks and expressions of how useful it has been to think through some of their current challenges. Everyone appears keen to renew their contract with the group.

7 The final stage

Like the initial stage of supervision, the final stage consists of two to three sessions. It is a time for taking stock, dotting i's and crossing t's, a time to "bring in the harvest", that is, to review, interpret, and absorb the results of supervision. If a final assessment is required it is done in this stage, partly for the benefit of the sponsor, who may have insisted on one in advance (this is especially the case in training supervision). There is little time to work on new learning issues. But if any remain, you and your supervisor can still look for other ways to address them.

What is more important now is to bring the long, intensive, and often ambivalent relationship between supervisee and supervisor to a satisfactory end. A highly personal, intensive working relationship of this kind deserves attention and a careful conclusion, simply to prevent the process of saying goodbye from adding any new traumas to existing damage caused by previous separations and splits from helpful outsiders.

7.1 We're nearly there

During the midterm review (section 6.2), you made or adjusted plans and agreements concerning the content of supervision and the methods used in the preceding period. Now you will be working towards ending the supervisory process. The final evaluation and time to say goodbye are coming into view.

Soon, you as a supervisee will have to continue independently. But you may wonder: am I capable of doing this and, if so, to what extent? It is time to explore this.

This review is guided by taking a (fresh) look at *what* you intended to learn in supervision. What has come out of this intention? In this context, you also look back at *how* the learning happened. What results have emerged from this relationship, this special form of learning aimed at developing professional competence?

Supervision and practice

Obviously, engaging in the formal supervisory sessions is an important condition for learning during supervision, but not the most important one. The outcome depends primarily on the supervisee's experiences and actions in practice, in between the sessions themselves. We can identify the following three actions:

1. The supervisee's first action is to review the supervisory encounter: do they remember what they said and contributed during the session? And do they recall how the supervisor (and any co-supervisees) responded? What does this mean for how the supervisee wants to think and act in future?
2. The second action concerns the actual follow-up in practice. Any follow-up is only truly meaningful if something has changed in the supervisee: a different perspective on (an aspect of) yourself must lead to a change in attitude and different behaviour in your work, otherwise the new insight would remain empty and meaningless.
3. The third action is the report that the supervisee gives at the next supervision session: what happened and how did it go? How do you evaluate your actions and experiences, and what is your conclusion? By (continually) accounting to yourself for the things you do and did, you assume responsibility for them.

In supervision (i.e. both the sessions and the practice in between), via a continuous stream of such actions, you can teach yourself to work (more) independently as well as, gradually, to carry out certain aspects of supervision on your own (an aspect called self-supervision or internal supervision by, for example, Casement, 2002).

What the supervisee should be able to do

The question of what the supervisee should now be able to do independently is not easy to answer, as doubts and ambivalence always play a role. In addition, this depends on factors such as:

- Is the supervisee a newcomer to this profession, or do you already have some experience in it?
- Has the supervisee had supervision before (if so, for how long and in what context) or is this the first time?
- Which phase of which professional training course is the supervisee in at present (e.g. undergraduate or subsequent degrees), or is supervision taking place in a different context, for example, as part of professional practice or as a requirement imposed by a professional institution?

- Which requirements and (assessment) criteria has the sponsor stipulated in relation to this supervision?
- What are the personal capabilities and limitations of this supervisee, that is, what can reasonably be expected of you at this stage and in this context?

Supervision is a personalised way of learning how to pursue a profession (more) independently, and this will of course be taken into account in assessing the outcome. However, this does not mean that no (minimum) standards should be imposed in this regard. The supervisee must have acquired some degree of independent learning from her own experiences and independent professional practice, else the supervisor may arrive at a firm recommendation for more supervision or training. How big "some degree" should be is difficult to say in general terms. This is normally considered on a case-by-case basis for each supervisee or situation.

7.2 Final evaluation and optional assessment

If the midterm review was prepared and conducted with care, the final evaluation—as a procedure—should not pose any significant problems. The supervision partners are on familiar ground (sections 3.3, 5.3 and 6.2). The supervisee writes another evaluation report as a basis for the subsequent evaluation session with the supervisor (and co-supervisees). The final evaluation is a review of the entire supervision period. Next, the outcomes of the supervisory relationship are assessed. Finally, this is followed by a look towards the future: how to continue on the established course?

The "harvesting", surveying the fruits of your labours via (self-) evaluation and hearing confirmation from your supervisor and co-supervisees, is normally a very useful and pleasurable experience. So it often prompts a wish to hold a modest "harvest festival", even if only in the shape of a biscuit with your tea or a posy of flowers on the table! There is significance in this natural urge to mark and enjoy it, and rituals such as these help in disengaging from the relationship. The harvest is often followed by a positive *assessment* of the supervision outcome by the supervisor. This is a critical moment, mainly because this judgement is associated with penalties: a pass in supervision means you are allowed to carry on, but a fail has consequences for the rest of your training.

Assessment

It may be useful to consider the term "assessment" for a moment. What does it actually mean and who is competent to do it? Assessment is based on *comparison*. According to the Concise Oxford English Dictionary, "to compare" means "to estimate, measure, or note the similarity or dissimilarity between". We then form a judgement and assign a qualitative value to that judgement. Some comparisons are objective, and others subjective:

- *Objective* comparisons are assertions based on facts. Those facts are or were observable, measurable or countable and, in principle, controllable. Because the content of assessment may entail a dispute over an assertion of the type "A equals B", it is mainly about the truth value of the judgement: the judgement is either true or untrue. Whether someone is right or wrong can often be demonstrated in these cases, so disputes can be resolved quickly.
- *Subjective* comparisons are about "I think" or "I believe". They are not (or are only partly) based on facts but much more on impressions and feelings. There is no question of being right or wrong, because everyone has their own experiences and is entitled to their own views and perceptions. Subjective comparisons are mainly about the quality of the judgement: we consider one thing to be better or worse than another. They are not necessarily *preconceptions*, in the sense of premature and unfounded opinions or viewpoints. Such preconceptions prevent us from actually understanding the things we hear, see, perceive, or experience. Preconceiving and prejudging can be counteracted by means of critical self-examination, willingness to confront oneself and a readiness to adjust one's own opinion.

Value judgements

The difference between objective and subjective comparisons is not always clear. Value judgements (as in supervision) often lie in the space in between.

Value judgements may have been based on *rules*: it is easy to determine which of two chess players is the better because the rules of chess are known and individual scores in a tournament can therefore be calculated quickly. In other situations, a value judgement is made by someone who is competent to do so on the basis of *expertise*. Expertise is gained through specialist training and professional experience. An expert's judgement is founded on basic principles (accepted by the professional group and training institutions) governing professional practice in the field. The judgement may have professional consequences as well, such as penalties or a need to do further training.

Qualitative or value judgements are not a matter of objective or absolute standards, but of *criteria* associated with proven results and expertise. In this context, therefore, we are concerned with assessments based on the supervision expertise of the supervisor and what quantitative research we have in the field.

Evaluation and assessment in supervision

Assessing achievements in supervision involves value judgements of the latter type mentioned above. This makes use of "competence based on expertise", possibly supplemented by a number of assessment criteria specified in advance, for example, by the sponsor. The question to be answered next is who is best placed to evaluate and assess the supervisee's personal learning process and results? Each of the partners in the supervision combination may have something useful to say:

a. the supervisee, especially when reflecting on personal experience;
b. the supervisor, aided by the supervision and training criteria;
c. the co-supervisees, who in any case have participated in achieving some of the outcomes related to supervision.

The supervision combination as a whole may therefore have acquired the necessary expertise. If so, the group is also capable of making a (sound) evaluation and assessment.

However, it is the supervisor who is responsible for the *final assessment* of the supervision outcome. This also applies to any reporting to the sponsor, in accordance with the agreed formal remit of the supervisor (see Chapter 2). It will therefore be *the supervisor* who, whether the final verdict on the supervision outcome is positive or negative, presents the supporting arguments (verbally or in writing) to those directly involved: the supervisee and the sponsor. In training supervision, it is often considered sufficient for the supervisor to complete a form. This is then processed and placed in the student's file. In the event of a difference of opinion over the final assessment, the student can consider an appeal; many training courses include this option and it is a requirement for formally validated courses. For the supervisor, it is important to pick up on such differences at an early stage and, where possible, to make them part of the assessment itself—for example, by stating both points of view and giving a personal final opinion taking all aspects into account.

Assessment based on a value judgement as part of a training or development programme is commonly called *summative assessment*, meaning that it serves the interest of external accountability. It sums up the learning of the trainee in the eyes of the developer. By contrast, ongoing assessment in the interest of the continual professional development of a professional is called *formative assessment*, meaning that it consists of an ongoing review and feedback to inform learning and development.

Assessment is becoming increasingly crucial in supervision, even outside the context of a practitioner's initial professional training. Professional associations and employers, and sometimes even client organisations, are increasingly insisting that the supervisor assess the supervisee formally on a regular basis, sometimes once a year, sometimes occasionally and upon request, for example on receiving an important promotion or acquiring a particular distinction or a new and challenging project.

Perspective into the future

A final evaluation in supervision is not complete unless combined with a longer-term perspective. This is closely related to the special dual nature of supervision:

- Supervision is about *learning from experience* within and for the benefit of independent professional practice.
- Supervision is also about *learning to learn* from experience in work and in life and "owning" this form of learning in such a way that aspects of it can later be continued independently (the "internal" supervisor; see for example Casement, 2002).

This means that, at the end of the supervision period, you need to consider the extent to which you are capable of this, the extent to which you can direct your own learning process. In other words: has the supervision also been used to further develop your "internal supervisor"? Then you can look at what you could do to continue your own learning process independently: learning from today to benefit tomorrow. This could be the final question you raise with your supervisor!

7.3 How do we go our separate ways?

In the beginning, at the start of supervision, the partners sought their own answers to the question of how to relate to each other (see Chapter 5). In parallel, it would appear self-evident that they should devote equal attention to exploring how to end well and go their separate ways. But this is often forgotten, sometimes out of clumsiness, or also because the importance of carefully rounding off a relationship is often underestimated or avoided because of hidden hurt from earlier separations. Perhaps you find saying goodbye difficult in general, and tend not to focus on it too much. On the other hand, a functional relationship is like any other relationship (see section 5.1) in that it involves an exchange of personal experience, deeply held feelings and vital insights. Ending such a relationship abruptly can cause unnecessary suffering and a reversal of what has been gained; whereas a conscious, shared process of preparing to say goodbye can be emotionally enriching for all concerned.

Saying goodbye

What do you have to say goodbye to after the end of supervision?

- First of all, of course, you are saying goodbye to the supervision itself: its objectives and the functional relationship. The final stage of the supervision period, with the final evaluation (if any) and subsequent assessment as its highlights, is dominated by a sense of completion. Anyone who has experienced this stage knows this, and can immediately recall how it feels: that's the end, it's over, thank you and fare ye well!

- Next, you are saying goodbye to each other: extricating yourselves from your personal involvement, the relational aspect of your alliance. If the supervision partners are likely to cross paths again elsewhere (which is especially likely in the case of fellow professionals in similar helping professions), saying goodbye to the here-and-now relationship and consciously "stepping out of role" can be very worthwhile: after all, the next time will be different in terms of involvement, content and situation. The next time the relationship may be more symmetrical, as with a collegiate, peer relationship.
- Supervisees who held an honorary or temporary post, as part of a placement or employment during their participation in supervision, should also say goodbye to any clients/patients/residents they have worked with. This also applies to colleagues and other professionals in the respective clinic, school or institution.

The question of how you should say goodbye is not so easy to answer. This depends so strongly on situational and personal factors that it is better left to the personal creativity, warmth and inventiveness of those involved or their nearest and dearest. It is generally recommended that the end be *marked*, possibly with some sort of acknowledgement or ritual, so that those involved not only know but also feel that the end has come. To say goodbye is to die a little, as the French say. It hurts and it does leave a wound.

Individual supervision can bring huge benefits to experienced practitioners as well. Equally, saying goodbye well remains difficult also for mature practitioners. The sheer fact that you know that there is a safe and protected space in your diary where you can raise thoughts about your work in helping conversations can bring immense support and relief. Experienced practitioners regularly bring their client work to supervision, as well as their managerial duties for others or their evolving relationships with peers and line managers. They trust that they can talk through the confidential details of their work and their own strong feelings, fears and even shame about their work with a helpful and supportive outsider, whom they know is fully on their side even if both are clear that supervisors view the material on its merits and without trying to flatter or mince their words. Supervision remains very challenging when your supervisor points out your vulnerabilities or agrees with you, for example, that you have exposed too much of yourself, were forgetful or made real mistakes. Nevertheless, looking at your own work with such tough, relentless scrutiny ultimately brings you relief and confidence, and makes you fitter in the same way as wearing out and testing your muscles makes your body fitter.

Case example

Nicolas has been working with his supervisor for a full nine years, and they have decided that it would be better for him to move on and find another source of help, for a variety of good reasons. Nicolas' practice is still developing into new areas, he would benefit from a fresh look at his work, plus his supervisor is now gradually retiring. Although Nicolas made this decision together with his supervisor quite a long time and many sessions ago, his feelings about the transition surprise him with their intensity. He notices that he has very mixed feelings, no trust in the other potential supervisors on his shortlist, and even real anger towards his current supervisor whom he often feels has "let him down" by calling the end. In the current year, the agreed ending has been referred to in every session, and both Nicolas and his supervisor avoid mentioning a date, seeming to want to postpone the finality of their collaboration. Things do not change until Nicolas finally starts interviewing other practitioners, mostly out of guilt and very mixed feelings including annoyance with his current supervisor. When Nicolas finally has a very thoughtful conversation with one of the other supervisors he comes back to his old supervisor with delight and some rather mixed reports about the other interviews. They keep working together for several more sessions, as Nicolas checks his choice for the new supervisor and gradually begins to see advantages in the new arrangement. For one thing, the new supervisor lives more locally. And he seems to have some interesting areas of expertise as well. The final session is like all the others, except that it is infused with great warmth and a touching friendship in the supervision combination. They give each other a long handshake at the final, long anticipated moment of ending. Nicolas is relieved to notice in subsequent years that he can still send his old supervisor an occasional email request and that he even receives an interesting referral as his supervisor is now definitely retiring.

8 The importance of writing in supervision

As we have seen in previous sections, supervision attaches a great deal of importance to writing: your aims, learning programme, work contribution, reflections and evaluations are usually reviewed both verbally and on paper. After all, not all work contributions lend themselves to spontaneous reproduction and free-flowing conversation (see section 3.3).

8.1 Work contributions are individually determined

Writing does not come easily to every supervisee. Many supervisees have a substantial resistance to writing, which can be overcome only with difficulty. However, writing for supervision is a skill you can learn, even though it does have its ups and downs. In supervision, writing is intended mainly for yourself and for this particular (supervision) situation—not for outsiders or for publication. You can't really go wrong!

No doubt you would be thrilled if this guide were to offer models, examples or schedules that you could then "fill in" in your own way. You might believe that you can "drive that train". But you would be mistaken. Presenting materials and work contributions in supervision is very remote from completing pro forma models but instead is a highly *personal account* of your own interests and concerns with regard to your practice or related to your supervision learning process. First and foremost, you as a supervisee write your supervision material for yourself. Then you share what you have written with your supervisor and co-supervisees so that they can help you to continue your learning process. Supervision is aimed at developing independence in your learning, thinking and working. However, this independence is only gained by allowing those others to intrude into your report and comment quite freely on what you have written. Having to overcome resistance to their "intrusion" is not unusual. You will therefore need to work out for yourself how you can remain open and curious in the face of your supervisor and possibly peers expressing themselves on your work. You want to shape your supervision process in such a way that you can be curious and excited about their views without being too precious about what you have reported. A guide like this can help to start you off, but the journey and your travels in supervision land are partly solitary, and your claim to independence within supervision and then also in your practice will have to be realised alone.

8.2 Reflective assignment

Now you have studied Part II of this book, you are probably able to formulate the first part of your learning programme in supervision. Bear in mind that the supervision will start soon or has already begun. You accept or set yourself an assignment: describe what you want to learn or the learning issue you would like to begin with right now. Look back at previous sections to see what is involved; you can find some tips for doing that in section 5.3. For example, search within yourself for an area for development, perhaps something that causes you doubts or lack of confidence regarding aspects of your work. Try to work this up into a learning issue that you can use in your supervision soon. Write some rough notes first and then a written work contribution of at least half a page.

8.3 Example of a writing problem

In section 6.3 we explained why reflecting in written form is important. It provides you with a tool for learning to think (more) independently and to organise your feelings, as well as for learning and working independently in your profession. After the supervision is over, you can then continue (provisionally) under your own steam; in a sense you become your own supervisor (however we would never advise going without supervision entirely, even though the frequency of sessions may diminish considerably).

It is true that many supervisees are more fluent with the spoken word than with the pen. They can find writing difficult so they sometimes try to convince their supervisor that verbal reflection alone might be sufficient or suits their learning style better than written reflection. Some supervisors will be insistent: they want to see something before they believe it. The following example illustrates what can happen then.

Case example: the supervisee who couldn't write

Amanda, a social worker who had had (individual) supervision before, came for group supervision with two other supervisees. She asked at the start to be excused from submitting written material, saying: "I can't write". Her previous supervisor had been sympathetic to this request, and that supervision had proved very useful. Even at work, she managed to keep her written reporting to a minimum. However, this time she was out of luck because the supervisor was not keen to immediately grant her a special status in comparison with the others. Moreover, written submission of learning material was a condition of the broader supervisory contract. And the supervisor added that this would give Amanda a chance to learn to write, or else to prove her case. Amanda and her co-supervisees agreed.

For the next session, the supervisor asked all three supervisees to try to write a reflective report on today's session, together with learning goals and desired outcomes. Amanda was allowed to limit her contribution to half a page. She was prepared to give it a try but apologised in advance for "the poor quality".

The agreed material was produced and the supervision group met for the second time. The supervisor started by discussing some written work contributions, coming to Amanda first to ask what she wanted to say about them. This part went well; Amanda's comments were to the point and an animated discussion ensued. The roles were then reversed and the focus shifted to "Amanda and her half-page". What she had written was great. But everyone, including Amanda, noticed that the verbal introduction she was asked to give took up a huge amount of supervision time. The supervisor suggested that Amanda halve that time in the next session by writing down her introduction and expanding her text by a quarter. She was happy to do that.

History repeated itself in the third session. However, during the discussion Amanda casually let it slip that she had "often filled whole diaries". The supervision session continued just as well as the first two. At the end, the supervisor suggested that the next time, besides producing an ordinary reflection report, Amanda could prepare her writing problem as a work issue and then present it orally. They could then take a look at it together and see if they could help her to get rid of the problem. Both Amanda and the others thought this was a good idea.

In the next session, the true nature of Amanda's problem finally emerged: it was not so much that she lacked writing ability, more that she was extremely bothered by an emotional block from her past. "What will "they" think of me?" was her big concern.

"They might misunderstand me, perhaps even laugh at me"; "I'm never sure if I can express my thoughts clearly enough for other people"; "Luckily, though, I can do it clearly enough for myself". To Amanda's amazement the supervision group did not respond like the "they" from her past, which confused her for a moment. But now her decision was made: she had had enough! By this time she was keen to be rid of the problem. But how? In response to a question from the supervisor, she promised she would try to find her own solution first. If and when she needed to, she could come back to the problem within the group. And once Amanda understood that she could relax and "write for herself" in supervision, she resolved to make writing a normal part of her routine.

Once she had done that, and after receiving some encouraging compliments, her writing went from strength to strength. It was not until the midterm review that she raised it again herself: "The problem is over now! It's just a pity I didn't tackle it sooner." Amanda was very relieved to have shed this emotional baggage. She could now focus all of her energy on the supervision, and she developed better file keeping at work to boot.

Conclusion

In this example, Amanda learned something important in supervision that she had initially wanted to keep outside the scope of her learning plan and objectives: she did not believe in the *mutability of a position previously adopted*: once you believe something, that is the end of it. "I can't write" was certainly a difficult problem for Amanda, but to the supervisor it also looked very much like clinging to a statement that the supervisor and co-supervisees were simply being asked to accept. However, they did not agree and started to negotiate. Amanda, though disbelieving, gave in; she would try to learn how to write, albeit with a warning about the consequences: "poor quality".

By taking this approach, a specific writing problem was resolved, or actually, generally good writing skills were allowed to surface in public. But an underlying problem was also brought to light and explained. Amanda's view of herself and the mutability of (fixed) opinions started to change as she learned to *reflect* more successfully. This stood her in good stead in the rest of her supervision. It also had a positive effect on her relations with teachers and fellow students on her training course, and with clients, colleagues, and others in her work environment.

Part III

Understanding the supervisory journey

You and your profession, including the theoretical underpinnings of supervision

The train has come to a standstill. The company has disbanded; the guide has said goodbye. Your journey of exploration has come to an end and hopefully you have made a lot of new discoveries. Perhaps you now think the supervision is over, but that is not entirely true: your experiences continue to evolve and pose questions. And hopefully you have acquired a taste for it, so much so that you'd like to go back and revisit some areas of particular interest, to see and experience them better. You have also learned how to continue travelling or learning independently, on your own initiative. A career filled with professional supervision beckons.

Part III is about this process of revisiting or "bending back", which as we saw in section 3.1 is one of the literal meanings of the word *reflection*. This part is intended for supervisees who want to take a look back after their substantial supervision experience. It may also inspire more advanced supervisees who seek a deeper exploration.

We suggest that the "areas of particular interest" which merit further investigation correspond with three core dimensions of supervision:

1. The first area that qualifies for further investigation is close to home; it is the person of the supervisee. In a sense, it lies within our own breast: *focusing on the inside* ...
2. The second area is something meaningful we have developed outside ourselves, it is the *profession* of the supervisee. This means taking another look at the aim of the journey; after all, we wanted to learn to practise our profession: *focusing on the outside* ...
3. Finally, we also want to take a look back at our faithful, trusty method of transport that, after all, managed to connect one with the other. We took the train (supervision), but could it also have been a jeep or a bicycle (a different form of continuing professional development)? *Focusing on the in-between* ...

9 The person

Although the title suggests that this section is about "the third person singular", it does of course concern *you* and all of you, but in particular you as a practitioner of your profession. You may or may not be (any longer) in supervision and/or considering working with another supervisor. Apart from being (= existing) and recognising yourself as being, the most pertinent aspects of you in this context are knowing, understanding, being able, wanting and doing. In supervision terms, we are going to look at your thoughts, feelings, wishes, and actions. Corresponding to these in your professional practice are, in the same order, *knowledge, attitude* and *skills*. In this chapter we examine this trio more closely.

9.1 Thinking and knowing

In section 6.1, which concerns the need for integration at the level of the person, we pointed out (based on experience) that there can sometimes be something wrong with the coherence between thoughts, feelings, wishes, and actions, that is, an incoherence or incongruence. As far as thinking is concerned, especially in connection with feelings, there is a lot more to say, as the following will show.

Autonomy thinking

For centuries, the prevailing view in Western culture has been that reasonable thought should be valued more highly than sensitive thought, including personal perceptions and emotions. This view is called *rationalism*: only through reason can man (learn to) know the truth. Rationalism is not the same as being rational. The latter could be defined as going about in a reasonable, considered and purposeful manner. As a school of thought, rationalism reached a peak during the Age of Enlightenment, which began in the seventeenth century and still has recognisable influence to the present day. Rationalism includes the Kantian concept of "moral autonomy" thinking (autos = self; nomos = law): the "thinking person" surveys the world and makes himself the norm of reality. What the "I" cannot comprehend through *reason* falls outside the scope of its thinking and is therefore unreal. A leading contemporary exponent of this school is the German philosopher Jürgen Habermas (1929-), who is attempting to modernise this conceptual framework, notably by seeking more connection with present-day reality by embedding rationalism in communication and a co-created reality.

Heteronomy thinking

It was not until the twentieth century that opposition to rationalism got properly under way. Now there was more emphasis on the fact that the I-thinker experiences only half of reality. This is because *the I* is counterbalanced by *the Other*. The other-ness of the "Other" is counter-balanced by the me-ness of the "I". Purely rationally, the I is not able to make contact, because contact requires more than understanding or knowing something. The only way to really learn to understand the other (another person) is to "set your mind to zero" now and then and to engage your sensitive capabilities. In other words, seeking contact means being interested in and developing an *affinity* with the other (i.e., people, but also in this tradition nature, art, even oneself, for example one's own irrational "shadow" sides).

Reason and sensitivity are afforded equal value in this relatively new critique of rationalism; both are equally necessary in order to approach reality in a meaningful way. Autonomy thinking should therefore be replaced by heteronomy thinking (hetero = the other; again the expression was coined by Kant). It is not the "I" who is the norm of knowing/understanding, but the "Other" who presents herself to me. I should therefore open myself up to the other-ness of the other, the other person. The French philosopher Emmanuel Levinas (1906–1995) argued convincingly for this and so did Martin Buber (1878–1965), while many new and contemporary schools of thought take heteronomy or "diversity thinking" as their starting point.

What is knowing and how do we acquire knowledge?

According to the Concise Oxford English Dictionary, "knowing" means being aware of something through observation, inquiry or information, but it also means having developed a relationship with something through meeting and spending time with it. In most European languages these two meanings are separate and there are two words for knowing—think about *"savoir"* and *"connaître"* in French and *"wissen"* and *"kennen"* in German. The first kind of knowledge leads to you becoming an expert, and the second one leads you to becoming a connoisseur. One is achieved through accumulation and analysis of facts about a phenomenon and the other through experience and exposure to the phenomenon itself.

To be able to acquire new knowledge under our own steam, we need a certain degree of independent, logical thinking. Logical thinking and reasoning is not the same as thinking and speaking based on common sense: a sort of practical wisdom that consists of a combination of intuition, instinct, and thought.

However, that wisdom (based on logical, practical thinking) often falls short so needs to be supplemented.

Logical thinking and reasoning

Logical, clean thinking is not just a question of being intellectually gifted; it is also a skill that you can learn.

You need to think independently to be able to solve problems independently. Logical thinking can help you to see the true connection between assertions and conclusion(s), and to study practical links between cause and effect. People may have problems, with themselves or their work, which can be traced to unclear thinking or errors in thinking.

Logical thinking is important for people who wish, in a professional way, to reflect, study, practise research, undertake training, run an organisation and/or work in a profession. Sharp, rigorous, and logical thinking is subject to formal rules. Devising and drafting these rules belongs to the domain of logic: the doctrine of the forms and methods of correct thinking and reasoning. The term "logic" is derived from the Greek "logos", which means "word" but also "reason" or "reasoning".

To find out more about this, consult the specialist literature; for our purposes, we suffice with a brief explanation and a few examples.

Using logical thinking we can determine, based on the truth of one or more statements, what else must then also be true. We can then make a reliable judgement on the question of whether a conclusion is true or untrue. Valid and correct reasoning always leads to a correct conclusion: if all of the assertions are true, the conclusion is also true; if the conclusion is untrue, not all of the assertions are true.

An example of valid/invalid reasoning:

Valid:	Invalid:
• All students are poor.	• All students are poor.
• I am a student.	• I am poor.
Therefore: I am poor.	Therefore: I am a student.

In the example of valid reasoning, the conclusion follows logically from the two assertions: I am one of them (a student) and therefore I am poor as well. In the invalid reasoning, the conclusion does not follow logically from what precedes it: not all poor people are students; there may be a different reason for my being poor.

An apt variation on this example might be:

Valid:	Invalid:
• I am a supervisee.	• I reflect.
• Supervisees reflect.	• Supervisees reflect.
Therefore: I reflect.	Therefore: I am a supervisee.

Here again: if I am one of them (a supervisee), I reflect. But if I reflect I am not necessarily a supervisee; philosophers reflect as well! The conclusion is not valid, because it does not follow from the assertions.

Note that the truth of the statements "all students are poor" and (all) "supervisees reflect" need not be addressed by the logician. That can be explored and determined elsewhere; logic is simply about the formal rules.

Sensible reasoning and argumentation

Sensible reasoning means having good enough reasons to support your opinion, conclusion, or judgement. Good reasons of this type can often be safely adopted from someone who is an expert in a particular field, in whom we have sufficient trust. After all, we do not all have to keep reinventing the wheel. What others have already discovered can often serve as a foundation for our own independent thinking.

Good reasons can also be derived from our own independent reflection, possibly aided by others as long as we do not succumb to "lazy thinking" (section 6.1). On the one hand, reasoning is about discovering or sharing truth; on the other hand, our aim in using reasoning is to convince the other person that our view is correct.

If errors of reasoning are made in this context (with or without awareness), they can be described as *sophisms*: deceitful arguments. These involve an incorrect presentation of facts, a distortion of the truth, an attempt to turn the truth to your advantage. After all, some people are interested in the truth only if it suits them! Sophisms are often used to avoid giving an answer, to achieve a particular goal or to "push through" a point of view where correct or honest reasoning has previously failed.

Some training in *making arguments* or *rhetoric* can therefore be very useful (for an overview of argumentation see Van Eemeren, Grootendorst, & Snoeck Henkemans, 2002; for a very readable introduction to rhetoric: Leith, 2011). Making arguments means justifying or substantiating your claims: "I think ..., because ..., since we agreed ..." or: "based on my opinion on ..." or: "as practical experience shows ...", and so on. Because arguments are intended to prevent or resolve differences of opinion, participants in a discussion are obliged to justify their claims, to support them with arguments. Opinion making is not blocked and is given a chance.

By reflecting in supervision through asking yourself questions you can also develop your powers of critical thinking, developing your thoughts into more than the above-mentioned opining based on "common sense".

Critical attitude

Thinking critically, including judging and evaluating, are among the core skills that every supervisee should acquire. Supervision is not just about developing the necessary technical skills; it is also about looking at those skills, thinking about them from a "once-removed" position. This requires honesty, truthfulness, and conscientiousness in handling (the ideas of) yourself and others. Within this it is particularly hard to develop self-criticism and a critical attitude towards your own views, your preconceptions and your own part in the causes of certain consequences, and yet doing so yields some of the most powerful fruits of supervision. You learn how to observe yourself differently and see different consequences of your skills, or motives behind them, something you can quite easily bring back from supervision to practice.

9.2 Feeling, longing, and relating

To practise a profession, of course, you need more than the right mentality, knowledge, understanding, thinking skills and critical attitude towards your own ideas and those of others (section 9.1). All of those form the general basis for proficiency or competence, but they are not the whole story. You learn to practise a profession only by using what you know and *doing* the work in a realistic context. *Proficiency* in the profession can be described as *both* having developed competence or expertise in something (by applying your knowledge in the practice), *and* having the right intention and motivation to work in the profession. The latter—"good intention"—includes a sense of purpose, which enables you to set yourself a particular objective and to aim to achieve it, possibly in stages.

Below we inquire into how you might develop the "right" intention, which includes appropriate feeling or care, a professional attitude and identity, and a positive motivation.

Feelings

Insight in helping conversations encompasses more than making good use of logic and knowing about the ins and outs of professional practice. Insight also comprises our personal experience in helping conversations, including feelings, hunches, desires, etc. (section 3.1). Feeling does after all mean picking up what touches us. Feelings include perceiving something, whether with our body, mind, or soul, that is, being sensitive, comprehending, being aware. A feeling is a mood or a particular inclination in which our (self-) understanding is being expressed.

In this context we are mainly concerned with feelings that can play a role in supervision and in professional practice, in both a positive and a negative sense. Some of these feelings are listed below:

- uncertainty and doubt about your own knowledge, preparedness and abilities;
- fear of the unknown or the unexpected; which can be felt as panic at the (first) shock of practice or an unexpected turn in helping relationships; or as "being in awe", not (yet) daring to attempt something difficult; or even as confusion and not knowing what to do;
- frustration caused by an inability to achieve something you would like to do, acquire or master;
- satisfaction on succeeding in a difficult task, especially if you are also complimented on it;
- resistance to change or something new, especially if it affects you personally;
- resentment of for example, your dependence on other colleagues (including, at times, supervisors) and their guidance or authority;
- anger with your supervisor, co-supervisee, colleague, manager, or a "difficult" client/patient/pupil;
- concerns and qualms about linking (practical) experiences to yourself or something that you yourself caused, or because of your intimate feelings towards a client;
- pressures around empathy, imagining yourself in someone else's position even if for example, they oppose you, or think or feel differently;
- happiness when someone else recognises your interests or concerns;
- liking or disliking someone because you see (too many) similarities with someone else that you know, or that you remember from your past as someone you liked or disliked;
- reluctance to do something you are not keen to do, although you are not definitely set against it; this includes "disclosure remorse" in supervision where you feel your openness has not been honoured or rewarded or has made your situation only more difficult;

• pleasure in encountering and working with (new) colleagues or supervision partners; being able to appreciate their sense of humour or companionship.

The ability to (learn to) practise your profession in a way that is personal to you depends on being prepared to identify your own feelings, and examine and revise them if necessary. Because *feelings* are strongly associated with or stem from your view of a person or thing, they can sometimes be revised by reconsidering your *view*, for example by interpreting certain facts differently. Your view of the matter can then change and, as a result, acquire a different emotional charge. Of course with particularly strong feelings this may be difficult and may take a long time in which you "work through" your appreciation of the thing and the feeling. Reflecting in supervision can be particularly useful in getting to know yourself better and also with a view to effect certain desired changes in your emotions and your experiencing.

Motivation

Motivation is about willingness to do what is expected of you in a job or profession. It assumes: I want to be here and do this, because I have a good reason for it, I have a positive attitude towards it. Motives often stem from ideals or values. This normally also applies to the motivation to pursue a particular course of study and/or a profession, although other influences may come into play as well in this decision. Once you have acquired a (provisional) motivation, you will quickly find that every profession centred on people is also governed by profession-specific ideals, values, standards, and views. Either you can embrace those values and views, or they dampen your wish to pursue it, and you make a different decision.

The main views, practices, and rules (of professional ethics and methodology) that govern actions in a particular profession can be discovered by looking at its philosophical framework and methodological principles. You can learn about these in your professional training and practice. It also makes sense to stay up to date by keeping abreast of the professional literature. How to integrate all of this (see sections 1.3 and 6.1) into everything you already are and have acquired, and how to shape your (initial) motivation into your professional practice, can be explored very usefully with the aid of supervision.

Professional stance

A specific basis for professional expertise lies in an appropriate stance towards professional challenges. One may define professional stance as a learned predisposition to react in a consistent way to a particular challenge. By this we mean a mental attitude or disposition in relation to something, for example yourself and your responsibilities, or your clients and how you need to welcome or receive them. Views, feelings, values, desires, opinions, and convictions all play an important role in a professional stance. Such a stance informs a particular way of acting, and even particular behaviours, or indeed it may inform their avoidance. In other words, a professional stance may refer to a particular attitude or set of views and evaluations at work within the person, which enable him to fulfil the meaning of his profession in a specific situation.

Professional identity

Professional identity is developed through training and by actually doing a job or pursuing a profession in practice: it is developed by acquiring the necessary integration of person and profession (sections 1.3 and 6.1). For a professional identity to form knowledge, skills and experience are instrumental but not sufficient. A professional identity is more than competence and preparedness; it is also a highly personal "moulding" of your professional stance. To speak about identity is to touch on a person's "essence": their being or their self, as they see themselves and would like to be seen, sometimes called their "signature presence".

After questions around motivation, skills, and knowledge have been resolved you will take up and form a professional identity over time, which makes you unique among other professionals. Your professional identity in turn will shape your practice in unique ways, with your own clients, specialty, and/or procedure within the wider professional norms. While a *reputation* is the external manifestation of professional identity, that is, how you are experienced by others, *identity* is also an inner experience where you experience yourself as remaining constant and equal to yourself (Erikson, 1968). Identity development takes place all the time but two stages are important in supervision:

1. From adolescence, when a person is seeking individual independence and their own place in society: *personal identity*.
2. During (further) training in order to develop professional competence, in personal attempts to identify with the professional group: *professional identity*.

In the case of trainee supervisees, the first identity is often still developing and the second is certainly so; development of the two identities can therefore coincide. In supervision, this sometimes leads to an additional focus on the person of the supervisee, who still has a lot to integrate in such a situation.

Conclusion

In conclusion, we could say that in supervision professional identities are formed and developed through reflection on thoughts, feelings, motivations, and attitudes. Such work can lead to a different understanding of yourself but also to a different view on the profession and the profession's role in society—all considered in close connection with your own role within the profession and larger society as well.

Views cannot be dissociated from attitudes. In a dynamic interaction and encouraged by continuing reflection, views can change which in turn influences our attitudes, feelings, aims and motivations. All together and in combination, these are the main preconditions for being able to act in situations where this is necessary and at the same time being able to learn continually.

9.3 Actions and skills

Before your action can be described as professional, more things have played a role than just thinking, feeling and longing. This often becomes clear only when there are mistakes, conflicts or incidents: usually important facts were not taken into account at the time; perhaps there was a lack of motivation; perhaps feelings got in the way, or a decision was made rashly.

Professional action is preceded by goals and intentions, but also by decisions: for example, deciding on the timing of an intervention or choosing between alternative approaches. Action also depends on the situation and available resources: if you want to buy a bicycle but have no money, you will have to defer the purchase; if you want to carry out a nursing procedure but lack the necessary funding, you will have to forego it; if you want to lead a team of professionals but have no idea how to gain acceptance, you will need to learn how first.

Actions and behaviour are not the same

Behaviour can be described as the (visible) way in which someone behaves: what he does and how he does it. Action informed by such behaviour means that someone can be held responsible for it and can therefore be asked why they did it. It will not always be easy to answer such a question: the action is sometimes caused by a reflex or informed by motivations that we are not aware of.

Like humans, animals display (reflex) behaviour, and they are unable to answer the question of why they do what they do. Being able to think about action and come up with an answer to such questions is what makes us uniquely human.

Action is closely connected with ability, the capacity to carry out certain behaviours in a technically correct manner. For this, you need to know not only *what* you need to do (content) but also *how* it should be done (methods, techniques). Proficiency in professional action therefore includes knowledge of both the act and the rules that govern it.

The profession and professional requirements

Having expertise or working professionally means acting methodically: with awareness, purposefully, systematically and procedurally (section 3.1). However, this does not mean that some skills cannot also be acquired with serendipity, by trial and error, or by deliberately practising something repeatedly. Experienced workers will be familiar with this. There tends to be a considerable contrast between how professional skills are developed (accidentally, erroneously) and how they are then applied (meticulously, deliberately).

The main aspects of what the practitioner needs to be able to do, what needs to be learned (from methodology or through action), and why, is prescribed in the first instance by the *professional community*. These things are different for a nurse than for music therapists, teachers, GPs, personnel workers, pastors, or social workers.

In addition, and partly on behalf of "the profession" although at a distance, it is the *professional training institutions* that set the tone. These institutions set out clearly and with authority what they believe the profession entails, what it should aim for, and how it should be practised.

In some professions, an important role is reserved for the *professional associations*.[1] This is especially the case where the concern is to contain, safeguard and quality assure the practice and practitioners including from the perspective of their clients, managers, and work supervisors in a particular occupational context. Professional associations also defend the interests of the profession, including professional standards and members' interests.

Taking into account the requirements for (entry to) your own profession, *supervision* is then an excellent learning tool to help you take a critical look at your conduct in that profession and to (re)discover your professional identity (section 9.2). It also teaches you how to learn from your experience.

Communication skills

In section 9.2 we referred to the wide variety of feelings that can play such an important role in communication between people. As a practitioner you need to work with such feelings and with an equally impressive body of knowledge. Your communication skills need to be tailored to your methodology and professional aims as you work, taking into account the pressures and emotions of the moment. You will be taught a range of skills that are relevant to your professional stance and actions, such as counselling skills (Heron, 1975). To develop and acquire a range of skills that are specific to your profession and that can be tailored around the moment of interaction with your client, you will find an initial impetus in the profession's methodology: in the lessons, literature and methodology training. Supervision builds on these skills and emphasises communication skills that go further and deeper, as you try to reflect on practical experience. Ultimately, if you can acquire the specific reflective skills of supervision, you will be able to continue your own learning process partly independently and to some extent become your own supervisor (Casement, 2002). What you have to learn in order to be an effective supervisee in supervision (section 3.2) is also relevant for your practice and continuing professional development.

Because functional communication is such an important element of professional practice, it may be useful to consider it for a moment. Basic skills are your ability to empathise with the other person, listen well, let your counterpart know that you have listened and empathised by offering summaries of what is important to them, ask questions, and give answers. Furthermore, you will need your ability to offer hypotheses and challenges to your counterpart and your sensitivity to *non-verbal* communication. In supervision, functional communication nevertheless has a strongly verbal emphasis. Holding conversations and picking up and processing relevant information is often at the core of the "helping" professions.

Verbal communication: questions and answers

An important part of verbal communication in this context is the asking of functional questions. Some people find it difficult to ask the right questions in a particular post and/or context. This can be to do with uncertainty about the purpose of your actions. It can also be linked to confusion about your position in relation to the person opposite you. The relevance of any questions to be asked depends on the position held by the asker and the purpose of the question: who is asking what of whom, why, when, in what situation, for what purpose? In theory and professional practice alike, the main problem is that the progression of thinking, and the actions based on it, depends on the extent to which the questions are appropriate and asked correctly. But which questions are useful? How do we formulate them correctly? And when do we give a good answer to questions? Some points to consider are outlined below.

a. The question

Before formulating a question, we should ask ourselves how we can obtain a good answer to the problem at hand. This could save others and us a lot of unnecessary trouble. Questions are a means towards achieving an end, for example, obtaining relevant information, preparing for an assessment, keeping a conversation going, helping someone to learn or come to a particular understanding. Questions also serve to meet formal criteria, depending in part on the intended goal: they should be formulated clearly and unambiguously, and be relevant and purposeful.

- If we want information about (controllable or empirical) facts, we can look for that intentionally, with a closed question. In these cases, simply answering the question fulfils the intention of the questioner.
- If we want to know someone's opinion, we should ask open questions, not questions that limit the answer or suggest the answer we want to hear. "What do you think of ...?" is an open question, whereas "don't you think that ...?" is not.
- If we want the other to learn and develop, it helps to be able to skilfully use a particular kind of open questions. There is a substantial difference between what we would call "I" questions and "Other" questions, the first being born out of curiosity or the need to arrive at some kind of "autonomy thinking" diagnosis. "Other" questions, on the other hand, are almost summaries of questions that your counterpart is asking herself at this very moment. Well-chosen "Other" questions have the propensity to move that thinking on by inviting the other person to think again about her own queries.
- Asking too many questions all at once can confuse the other person, keeping him or her from giving a good answer. Even an exchange of questions and answers can unduly inhibit good reflection, because the questions are experienced more as a "cross-examination" than as an invitation to reflect and explore.

- You can also move a good conversation on just by offering encouragement to say "more", for example, by saying, "tell me more about that ..." or by repeating a noun with a questioning inflection: "the police?", or even by offering an hypothesis about what the other person wants to say next: "it sounds like you are having doubts about that interview coming up"; although, in that case, be prepared to be contradicted as well.

b. The answer

What can we do if we find ourselves in the position of answerer—like we are very often in supervision? In any case, we should be aware that questions are always based on preconceptions (prior knowledge, values). Questions come from somewhere and have a purpose; the questioner is aiming to achieve something such as deeper understanding, checking an idea about what is going on, wanting to show you an alternative way of looking at things.

Questions are *value*-driven: for the asker, the question is based on a value judgement; he wants to achieve something that is important to him. For example, someone asking why smoking is bad for one's health might find the answer important in deciding whether or not to stop smoking.

Questions are also *knowledge*-driven: the asker wants to know something that he does not know as yet, but about which he has suspicions: the smoker already knows about the potential link between smoking and health, and is now seeking more specific details. Alternatively: someone asking how to travel from A to B already knows that there are two places called A and B, that it is possible to travel from A to B, and that there are different ways to do that.

c. The topic of conversation

In all professional communication, the first question to ask is: *who is talking to whom* and *what are they talking about*? To stand the best chance of a productive interplay between question and answer, we need to have agreement on what the topic is and what we are aiming for. Has the issue or topic been clearly stated or described?

- For example: if we agree that we are talking about a horse, questions can be asked and answers given about characteristics or qualities of horses and/or my horse Blackie. If it is not clear that I am talking about Blackie, my interlocutor might think I am talking about her cat Sooty; after all, both animals are black and are pets.

- Another example: if a supervisee's work contribution concerns a complicated relationship problem with a client from a different culture, and that fact is not mentioned at all in the supervisee's contribution, there is a strong possibility that the conversation will be about handling relationship problems in general and that the supervisee will not learn to take culturally determined aspects into account in their approach. As a consequence, the client may feel misunderstood and drop out. Hopefully the supervisor will notice in time!

Joint agreement of the topic is important but may still be problematic for example, where the partners *do* agree on the topic of their conversation but make a joint error on the basis of an *incorrect assumption*.

For example, if two people see something white hovering above a swamp at twilight, they may think it is a ghost. Their conversation is about ghosts, especially that one there, and they fret about ghosts and all of their negative connotations. In such a situation, both asker and answerer lose their way: they have lost track of reality and start to "hover" themselves!

"Ghosts" like these crop up a lot in communication; if noticed, they can often be surprising or amusing. Sometimes there only needs to be a comma or other punctuation mark in the wrong place in a sentence for the meaning to become unclear; in a spoken sentence, the interpretation often depends on the tone of voice. The reader or listener "hovers" if they are not sure precisely what the writer or speaker wanted to say, and then they fill it in for themselves.

For every functional conversation, therefore, an initial requirement is that the *purpose of the conversation* should be clear to all participants and, where necessary, made explicit. This avoids any figurative discussions about ghosts or people beginning to "hover". Apart from the topic of conversation, the terms used should also be clear, or be made clear, to everyone.

Pay attention in particular to terms that have different meanings and can therefore lead easily to misunderstanding. For example, do terms like "contracting", "assessment", or "supervision" mean the same to all participants? By now it will be clear to readers of this book what is meant by the term "supervision", but in some other countries and in commercial settings the supervisor is also (still) seen more as a regulator or watchdog. So don't be too quick to assume that other people immediately understand what you mean by certain terms (especially if those terms are very familiar to you).

Another requirement for an effective conversation is to take account of the connection between a question and the problem to which an answer is being sought. A too-long or too-complicated question can be broken down into sub-questions, in which case the answer can also be given in sections. If the distinction between main question and sub-questions is not clear, the question can be reworded or divided up differently. To put it briefly: in order to answer a question appropriately, we first need to examine the question itself. In other words, and according to a well-known saying, "look before you leap". What do I want to know and how do I ask that?

Problematising work issues

Finally, and further to our earlier comments on problematising (section 3.2), we would like to add the following. Problematising is not only relevant to the developing of work contributions in supervision; it is at least as important in addressing work-related issues in practice. Working professionally requires you to find an appropriate answer to the problem at hand based on effective and targeted questioning.

In other words: you first need to know what is going on before you try (ideally together with others) to find a solution. The following list of types of questions may be helpful:

- "What" questions: looking for facts.
- "How" questions: looking for procedures.
- "Who" questions: looking at someone's state of mind and emotions.
- "Why" questions: looking for causes, motives.
- "What do you think" questions: looking for opinions.
- "For what purpose" questions: looking for (someone's) intentions.
- "What next" questions: looking for a solution.

The answers obtained to questions like these provide more insight into the problem. Making the here-and-now specific can bring a solution closer. In addition, the seasoned practitioner will be able, drawing on many specific problems, to generalise: what is generally true about this specific problem, that is, what do I know is occurring in other similar cases? Exploring this question further, for example for the purposes of research and policy-making, can lead in the end to a general improvement in aspects common to many problems in practice.

Case example of how ideological views on the person make a difference

The supervisee worked as a senior accountant and advisor in a global accountancy firm and had moved (part-time) into internal leadership development and leadership coaching within the firm. After she completed her coach training she has contracted a supervisor to talk through her client work and her developing coaching practice. The firm's philosophy being what it is, closely aligned with enlightenment ideas and rationalist, autonomy thinking, she found herself using quantitative questionnaires to review her coaching practice. At one point in supervision she requested to talk about the results of her evaluations and she expressed some concerns about one client's marks, which seemed a little lower than those of other clients. At that point the supervisor challenged her. "These are the marks of your clients. How are they relevant to you? What marks would you give yourself in your work with them?" The supervisee was baffled and took some time thinking about what to say ... "Well, they are my clients so my marks would be the same as theirs. These marks tell me how much they as the key beneficiary of coaching have taken from our sessions". After this the supervisor spoke about her own practice: how on several occasions she would give herself excellent marks although her clients' marks or feedback had been poor; and vice versa, how on some occasions she received high praise but would rate herself much lower. The latter were occasions where she thought she had been "coasting", or in other cases "struggling" to come to a deeper understanding of the client's issues.

They embarked on a philosophical conversation about the objectivity of feedback and whether anyone has the "right" view on the quality of helping conversations. What would a "heteronomy" view on the usefulness of feedback be? On the one hand the personal view of the client has to be fundamental, and on the other hand such a view is subjective and itself influenced by the client's ongoing learning process and difficulties.

The supervisee was initially quite shaken in her beliefs and returned to the conversation in this session many times over the next several years. She said it had opened her eyes both to think about who decides about the quality of her work, and on the limited availability or relevance of quantitative, hard feedback in helping conversations. On a personal level the conversation had liberated her to be more "herself" in helping conversations: more authentic and freer in her interventions.

10 The profession

This chapter is about why you, *the person*, picked this book up in the first place: practising in *the profession*. We will take a moment to clarify this. After all, it is about (the background to) your own (future) job or profession, that is, your practice, and ways of thinking about it. In the previous chapter (sections 9.1 and 9.2), we looked at thoughts, feelings, attitudes, and skills; now we hope to shine a fresh light on theory and practice, thinking and working.

10.1 Professional theory: thinking about the profession

Contrary to what the title might suggest, this section is not specifically about your own profession. You can find plenty of information on that in your specialist literature, possibly supplemented with theoretical content from your professional training. This section offers more general reflection, which you can translate to the circumstances in your own professional context. The Oxford English Dictionary defines a profession as "a paid occupation, especially one that involves prolonged training and a formal qualification". A *profession* is practised or pursued, and you can be trained for it; a *position* is a task, role, or post mostly within a profession in a specific working situation.

Interaction between profession and training

Jobs and professions are gradually being influenced by three sources: the social institutions, new trainees coming through, and the clients helped by the profession.

Supervision moves within the field of tension between professionals and professional practice and lies at the heart of change in the professions: what does the work entail and how should it be carried out?

- Professional care institutions operate on the basis of particular views about what needs to be done and how the work here and now must be done.
- Training institutions—and also this book!—operate based on their own particular views of what *should* be done and how, which does not always tally with the views and procedures in professional practice.

For supervisees, this can lead to an irritating dilemma: sometimes they have to choose one view and sometimes the other. The question is, which views should set the direction of supervision: the views of the training institution or those of the employer, the views of their teacher or those of their supervisor, general theoretical views or those taken from their practice? Is there a solution to this dilemma?

- Where the training view is dominant, the supervisee is learning to work on the basis of this framework (top-down thinking and working).
- Where the practice view (institution's/employer's/client's view) sets the direction, the supervisee is learning to handle and integrate a range of views flexibly in their professional practice (bottom-up thinking and working).

With good coordination between training and practice and between supervisor and supervisee, based on appropriate supervision within the institution or work context, a solution to any professional dilemma is normally found. In principle, such new solutions will also help to clarify and handle similar dilemmas, for other (future) practitioners.

The above shows that *supervision cannot be neutral*. Supervisees will have to find their way in the field of tension between views in training and views in practice. The supervisor can help with this. It can therefore be useful in supervision to pay some attention to overarching philosophical or ideological views ("theories of man" or visions of humanity) within the supervisee's context. By this we mean general views which partly define the profession and which influence opinions about working in professional practice. Let's look at a few of such overarching, integrating views.

Direction-setting views

Views within the supervisee's professional context are themselves partly determined by their integration within broader conceptual frameworks. Often, views from outside are responsible for determining the position of a job or profession, as practised in the more general socio-cultural context of the particular society. Changes in that context can have consequences for the prevailing opinions within a professional group, for example, concerning objectives, methods, required capabilities, or policy with regard to tackling problems (see, for example, Foucault, 1961, for a contextual study of some of the "helping" professions in the enlightenment era).

In this setting, "socio-cultural context" means the position that a job or profession occupies within the total complex of institutions in (sectors of) society. There are many people-oriented jobs and professions in which supervision plays or can play a role; they are often practised in one of the following sectors:

- healthcare (nurses, doctors, paramedics);
- mental health (psychosocial care providers, clinical psychologists, psychotherapists, psychiatrists, art and play therapists, etc.);
- social work (social and socio-cultural workers, counsellors, creative therapists, staff of special facilities for young people, the elderly, women, the physically or mentally challenged, addicts, etc.);
- pastoral work (priests, pastors, pastoral workers, etc.);
- education (teachers, pupil counsellors, remedial teachers, school counsellors, school management, etc.);
- personnel work and employment matters (occupational health employees, psychologists, employment lawyers and mediators, HR and leadership-development experts);
- personal and organisational development (organisation-development experts, executive coaches, advisers, consultants, mentors, facilitators and leadership tutors);
- the judicial system (child and youth protection workers, staff of rehabilitation centres or penal institutions);
- intramural and other residential facilities (workers providing support for children, young people, women, the elderly, mixed-age groups, assisted living, crisis shelters, etc.).

Thinking about our place in society

In the following pages we take a closer look at the sources of direction-setting and ideological views, and the philosophies from which they derive. For the helping professions, the various different views of man and society are particularly important. A vast amount of literature is available on this. It is however possible to distinguish two major schools of thought or philosophies that underlie much of this thinking: autonomy and heteronomy thinking (in other words, positivism/objectivism versus constructivism/subjectivism). Directly or indirectly, philosophies have important consequences for views in different professional contexts, which is why it is so important to reflect at this abstract level. We touched on the relevant distinctions in section 9.1 but will now examine them in more detail.

Thinking about man and society has a long history in our culture. Its origins lie in Ancient Greece when, around 500 years before the Christian era, thinking about the universe and nature began to shift towards a greater focus on man and his (political) environment. This later served as a foundation for Plato, Aristotle (fourth century BC), and others in building their own system of thought which captivated many and still has considerable influence to the present day. This lasting influence was possible because emerging and increasingly influential Christianity incorporated the main ideas of Greek thinking into its own doctrines. In the Middle Ages, Christian theology was the dominant school of thought in what is now called "Western" culture.

Rationalism

It was not until the seventeenth century that Descartes (1596–1650) devised new insights from which modern scientific thinking could develop. The main innovation in Descartes' thinking was the idea of the division between mind and matter, the spiritual and the physical. This division enabled the natural sciences and the humanities to develop separately.

Descartes and his followers also carried this *dualistic thinking* over into their ideas about humanity. They regarded intellect and reason as the highest human virtues. The physical and material served merely as a vehicle; emotions and the senses were not reliable because they could deceive the intellect. This school of thought resulted in the rationalism of the *Age of Enlightenment*, which reached a peak in the nineteenth century. According to rationalism, not only things, facts and events were regarded, treated, or studied as objects or themes; so were people and so were their social relationships. The individual, personal and subjective aspects of human beings and their relationships were declared subordinate. The latter idea did provoke growing opposition but it was only in the twentieth century that the inadequacy of rationalism began to be more widely recognised.

Humanism

The modern Enlightenment philosophy, with its optimistic faith in progress or belief in human (technological) ability, also offered space for humanism to grow as the staunch defender of human reason and values. The core idea in modern humanism became that, while human ingenuity was capable of all sorts of technological achievements, these scientific improvements could do little about the growing dissatisfaction within the populace and was therefore unable to resolve suffering, social unrest and political problems. In the nineteenth century this finding led to the emergence of several *human sciences* such as sociology, anthropology and psychology. This list was further differentiated and expanded in the twentieth century. The general (positivistic) expectation was that, guided by reason, the human or humanistic sciences would begin to improve the human condition in the world and increase the sum of human happiness.

Crisis

Although the trend towards humanism and the humanities (social sciences) did produce a series of successes, the original expectations were not entirely fulfilled. For many, precisely the contrary was the case and humanism found itself in crisis. Kierkegaard and Nietzsche showed that the positivistic optimism of faith in progress could not supply an answer to crises in meaning and, with the twentieth century existentialism of thinkers such as Sartre and Camus and the horrors of the Second World War, the crisis only deepened.

Observers rightly asked the question: How could humanism have failed to achieve its ideals despite such an extensive arsenal of humanities and social sciences (and all of their applications)? What was humanism lacking? Modern-day thinkers attribute many of those failures to rationalism and positivism. Autonomy thinking, with a strong emphasis on objectification, generalisation, totality, and uniformity (unity at the expense of diversity), is not, in their view, in a position to make real contact with man as a subject. People (instinctively) do not wish to be treated as objects or a (general) theme; they want to be known individually and personally, in their own unique and current self-experiencing or subjectivity.

Humanism did not emerge from these crises unscathed. However, after the Second World War it enjoyed a resurgence in the social sciences in the guise of "humanistic psychology". This time, the subject and the highly subjective human emotions and tensions were embraced as the focus of study, and personal experience, growth and self-actualisation were elevated to goals, with the focus being more on the practice of personal counselling and therapy than on generalisable empirical research. Carl Rogers and Abraham Maslow were the first advocates of this school of thought, which is still important today in the study of helping conversations.

Objectification

Contrasting with this tradition within humanistic psychology, an objectifying view of humanity and society can still be seen within the humanistic sciences: "the" person is observed, studied, instructed, healed, helped, educated. Man and society are "steered in the right direction", and what is right is determined "objectively".

In such a philosophy, observers, teachers, physicians and others often sincerely believe that empirical and generalisable research is the best way to find "the" truth about something, and that they are justified in imposing their own views, conclusions and will upon others because "I'm doing this for your own good". In a sense, their answers precede the other person's questions; the other person is seen as an object with nothing (or, nothing objective) to contribute. The professional is in fact holding a monologue with himself; the other person acts only as a trigger. Rationalism/objectivism (autonomy thinking taken to the extreme) can lead to *totalitarianism*: seeking to rule or control based on a central philosophy, idea, or conviction. Totalitarianism occurs not only in (party) politics; it can also be identified in (doctrinal, sectarian and/or fundamentalist) religions and social movements, ideological institutions and closed communities.

Diversity as an alternative?

In a more modern humanistic philosophy in which diversity is a basic principle, people are less interested in uniformity, objectivity, and the dominance of their own opinions. "Diversity thinking" or heteronomy thinking starts with the other person and ends in *pluriformity* (a greater focus on variety than on the uniform, the communal). Anyone who takes the subject seriously is interested in the other person and listens to what concerns or interests them, their experiences, what they believe is worth mentioning and what they want to achieve. The answer follows from the other person's question, rather than preceding it. A dialogue becomes possible which leads to shared reflection (see De Haan, 2012, Chapter 3, on reflective dialogue in supervision). Whereas *monologues* belong with the active, objectifying and controlling "I", a *dialogue* invites the subjectivity of the other person to share in the "I", within a personal relationship taking shape right here and now. This creates opportunities for bridging the gulf between people.

At the same time, subjectivism (heteronomy or "diversity" thinking taken to the extreme) can also lead to chaos (disorder) and anarchy: unfettered independence of every individual. Uncontrollability is the result, and people become entangled in a "war of all against all" as the British philosopher Thomas Hobbes (1588–1679) called it in his book *Leviathan*.

A compromise

A radical choice of autonomy or heteronomy thinking can therefore never produce the "egg of Columbus". An ordered society cannot function without uniform laws, objective empirical research, and rules that apply to all. But equally, a society cannot function properly if it does not leave enough space for the individual, if exceptions from the rule are not permitted. The French philosopher Levinas (section 9.1) called this the "drama of politics": justice for all can lead to injustice for an individual. As a result, it will usually be necessary to find compromises: in governing the country, in resolving conflicts in society, in professional bodies and institutions and even in your own professional practice. In the world of helping conversations, an example of such a unique and workable compromise is the contract between client and service provider, or between supervisee and supervisor.

Conclusion

By now it will hopefully be clear that philosophical ideas and ideologies are influential, that they have many and varied dimensions, and can have consequences for professional practice and the stance taken by practitioners (section 9.2). It is therefore useful to be aware of the particular view of our place in society that is adopted and applied in your chosen profession. On what basis are treatment, learning, and other objectives determined, and why is the work (mostly) done in a particular way? And how are the people in the helping professions treated? Why in this way and not in others? How do you want to do it yourself? Bear in mind that, in order to move towards different behaviour or a different way of working, a turnaround in thinking may be needed: from bottom to top, from top to bottom, or a bit of both!

10.2 Professional practice: working in the profession

From your training and the specialist literature, you will probably already know about specific answers to general questions that everyone asks, such as:

- Why do we exist? (legitimacy of the profession/field of work)
- What are we here for, what do we want? (objective)
- What should we do? (policy and code of conduct)
- How should it be done? (methods)
- What means do we have at our disposal? (people, funds, and other resources).

The particular responses to these questions are direct sources for the "direction-setting or ideological views in the supervisee's context" (see section 10.1). On that basis and within that working context, you will attempt to find or redefine your position within the profession.

Supervision and observation

Because supervision often draws from the communicative aspects of the helping professions (see section 3.2 and chapters 9, 10 and 11), we highlight another aspect of it here, namely *observation*. Observation is an extremely important element of our communication with others: what do we perceive? what do we see? what do we hear? what do we experience? what do we believe? what do we intuit? After all, it is the source of everything that we believe or assume to be "true".

Here is a well-known quotation about observation, by David Bohm, spoken in his lecture at the University of California, Berkeley, on 6 April 1977:

Reality is what we take to be true. What we take to be true is what
we believe. What we believe is based upon our perceptions. What
we perceive depends upon what we look for. What we look for
depends upon what we think. What we think depends upon what
we perceive. What we perceive determines what we believe. What
we believe determines what we take to be true. What we take to be
true is our reality.

As the quote illustrates, observation is in large part a circular process
where thoughts are confirmed by observation, observation is confirmed by thinking, and anticipation or pre-judgement reigns. It is hard
work to look for freshness in perception and to find instances where
we observe something new and unanticipated, and do not overlay it
with our pre-existing expectations. We all succumb at least in part to
the so-called "hermeneutic circle" (Heidegger, 1927) where all that we
can see has been determined by our frameworks of seeing, our past
experience and expectations, and our own interpretive powers. It is not
a gross overstatement to conclude that the whole of our understanding is already pre-determined, namely by all the parts and instances of
our understanding, which in turn are also pre-determined, namely by
the whole of our understanding, and so we are (at least in large part)
perpetually locked in cycles of confirmation that screen out genuine
observation and wonder.

Gadamer (1975) further developed this concept of a hermeneutic
circle. While Heidegger saw the hermeneutic process as cycles of self-
reference that encapsulated our understanding in *a priori* prejudices,
Gadamer took the hermeneutic circle more as an iterative process
through which a new understanding can indeed be developed by means
of exploring and appreciating the detail of existence. Gadamer viewed
fresh understanding as linguistically mediated, namely through conversations with others. In conversations reality can be explored from
different hermeneutic circles and an agreement can be reached that rep-
resents a new understanding.

Conceptualisation

If observations can occasionally be used to arrive at fresh understanding, then we are not just finding a new insight but we are also,
at the same time, changing our conceptualisation. We are constantly

perceiving our observations and (self-) understanding from within an interpretative framework. When something changes in our observations or understanding, our framework has to shift as well in some way.

Generally, conceptualisation is a process by which each of us shapes our own world, or the situation here and now as we experience it. We create for ourselves an idea of the world in which we live. We make a sort of model or map of the world on which we then largely base our actions. Any fresh modelling is based on old models that are very resilient and is therefore prone to serious limitations that conversations and sharing of understanding may mitigate. Biases or limitations in new understanding stem from the following sources:

- Perceptual biases: our senses (sight, hearing, touch, taste and smell) can deceive us and our selective attention may look for confirmation rather than fresh observation.
- Social biases: we often wear "coloured glasses" due to misinterpretations, group pressures, or preconceptions.
- Individual biases: we filter reality based on our personal history, a wide range of experiences/perceptions, and our own interpretation of them.

It is the personal filters in particular that underlie profound differences between people. They are however very useful in supervision as different people will see different things and by having a difference in observation we open up the possibility of new learning.

Conceptualisation through language

Gadamer (1975) drew attention to the importance of language in the possibility for the hermeneutic circle to be generative. The use of language in reflecting about your work and your observations is crucial, both in your own sense making and in the conversations with your supervisor. Using language, we create ideas (models, conceptualisations) of our experiences and of the world, but we also use language to present our ideas and offer them to others. This sense making is influenced by three important processes: generalisation, deletion, and transformation, which are outlined below.

a. Generalisation

A specific experience serves as a model for a whole category of similar experiences. For example: after an uncomfortable experience with expressing feelings to your supervisor, you might (unconsciously) adopt the principle: "never show your feelings in supervision". However, as a principle for the future this conclusion might go very wrong (as it may limit your work contributions in supervision); moreover, this idea might put you at a disadvantage in other relationships as well, for example, with your next supervisor. The experience has been wrongly generalised. Both negative and positive experiences can be wrongly generalised.

b. Deletion

This means the omission of (important) observations or ideas when conveying experiences. For example, you "play deaf" to parts of someone else's story, or you "forget" part of your own. Selective listening and speaking is something we all do. It can sometimes be useful (e.g. as a protective measure) but in our professional practice we should be able to handle it with awareness. If your client is (unconsciously) withholding certain information, you may intuit something important that may help in understanding the client's issues much better.

c. Transformation

In transformation, connections between parts of someone's "model" are presented differently than might be assumed. All sorts of defensive routines such as rationalisation, suppression, and distortion are essentially such transformations.

A frequent example in supervision is presenting an ongoing process as if the event has already ended. For example: "I regret my decision", rather than: "I had to decide on …; however, I think I made a mistake; I can reconsider it." Another example: "John's fear of spiders is just an oddity", rather than: "John is (currently) afraid of spiders; it doesn't need to stay that way".

The usefulness of conceptualising

Helping conversations are occasional or repeated communicative interactions between people in which information, insights, feelings and opinions are exchanged. Concepts can help in developing someone's personal perspective on how people in interactions handle themselves, their situation, and other people. A theory is often useful because it provides a conceptual framework that can help in analysing and clarifying such interactions.

For some professions, it is enough to use interactions purposefully, for example, in library work, shops, information and advisory services, pharmacies, and certain medical or paramedical jobs. For other professions, however, this is not enough. In those professions you are also expected to use relationships in a functional way. Following on from our earlier comments (sections 3.2, 5.1, and 6.1), we examine this in more detail below.

Using a relationship

To be able to use a relationship, you will first need to have one! How does a relationship come about? A relationship is a temporary or longer-term emotional connection between people in which experiences, insights, feelings, and opinions are exchanged. For personal relationships, such an exchange may be enough and ongoing, as such relationships are an aim in themselves. Functional relationships, however, are not an end goal but are focused on an aim associated with their task, such as service provision or a personal learning process.

Perlman (1957) writes that close links develop between people as a result of shared, emotionally charged experiences. In the private sphere, where relationships are often experienced as self-explanatory, this can be very beneficial for the emotional growth and development of both children and adults. This benefit of relationships is also used in the professions and jobs that are focused on helping others. According to Perlman, all growth-promoting, helping, and teaching relationships have the following four elements in common:

- *Acceptance*: I accept you as you are, as well as your humanity and uniqueness. But I don't need to agree with you on everything; sometimes I even reject or deplore your behaviour.
- *Good faith*: I have confidence in you; I believe you are capable of developing and changing yourself.
- *Beneficence*: I encourage you to continue on your journey and will help you as much as I can.

- *Intended outcome*: Professional relationships are also characterised by a conscious *focus on a contract with objectives and goals*.

Clearly the ability to intentionally develop, or learn to develop, good relationships for the purposes of helping and teaching is crucial in the helping professions. The supervisory relationship itself can serve as a model for other helping relationships in the supervisee's practice. The idea of such a high-quality, "good" relationship in the helping professions is often expressed by Greenson's (1965) term "working alliance"—a concept that Bordin (1979) further subdivided into:

1. Agreement on the aims of the relationship, that is, agreement on what the relationship is there to achieve, including goals and objectives ("agreement on goals");
2. Agreement on the interpretation of the tasks of the relationship, that is, agreement on how partners work together, including the responsibilities of both parties ("agreement on tasks");
3. Reasonable strength of the rapport or affective connection between the participants in the relationship ("bond").

In practice, however, a good "working alliance" may mean a few other things as well. We can safely assume that in a good, functional, working relationship we can expect a reasonable amount of affection, mutual understanding, agreement on what, why and how to work together, trust, safety, mutual respect in terms of competency and capability, and "grit" or fearlessness in the ability to challenge.

Entering into and developing relationships is of course mainly learned by being in very intimate relationships from earliest childhood, but this basic understanding can be enhanced by knowledge about relationships and also through action. For example, in a learning environment such as supervision, you can develop your relational competence and also remind yourself how it feels on the "other side" of the helping relationship. Supervisees sometimes notice that they are troubled by personal experiences that inhibit their relating or learning. If they bring this up for discussion, they can discover that the facilitative and personalised way of learning in supervision is a good counterbalance. They can learn how to handle these sensations in such a way that they no longer inhibit their work but can even be put to use.

Helping relationships

Like supervisory relationships, all helping relationships (between the practitioner and the people they are serving) are based on *inequality* (section 5.1). Helping relationships are focused on an objective defined by the task. Partners bear their share of responsibility for achieving that objective. Even though most of the responsibility for outcomes is usually with the client, this does not mean that the helper does not carry any. The old coal man's trick of saying to his lad: "You carry the coal up those stairs, then I'll carry the responsibility!" would not work nowadays, and such inequality entails aspects of power and authority: abuse of power is not far away. Essentially the responsibility of the helper consists in keeping the process and relationship on track, helping the other within that relationship, and reviewing the contract and process at regular times.

Power and authority

When engaging in helping relationships, we should be prepared for their inherent *power aspects* (see also section 2.3). Power can be described as the ability to influence others' behaviour, to steer the other person in a particular direction. Exercise of power features in many relationships and can be handled in different ways. Power can be distinguished from *authority*, which is *legitimised power*. Someone in a job or profession has a certain power, but also authority and hence "permission" to exercise that power, both over the other person and for his benefit. The other person knows this and (usually) accepts it; it is part of their (implicit) contract.

In a functional teaching or helping relationship, moreover, it is not just the professional who can exercise power over the client, student or supervisee (there is always power the other way round, the power of volition expressed by for example, attending, going along with exercises, or sticking to the contract) yet the professional does in the end hold the balance of power.

Problems in *handling power* can be avoided if that power is not obscured by the professional but is opened up for discussion. Potential opposition can be clarified in open communication. To avoid becoming entangled in power struggles or giving an impression of abusing power ("I rule the roost here, so jump to it ..."), you would do well to be frank about the *power aspects* and to assume responsibility for them. An *abuse of power* exists only if the professional is pursuing private goals rather than utilising her position for the other person's benefit.

A power balance based on inequality should always be focused on the interests of the person who is rightly making an appeal to you within a functional relationship. There is a vulnerability in making such an appeal and (particularly also in supervision) opening up areas of concern or doubt, and this vulnerability needs to be honoured and ideally also named. Ultimately as a practitioner in the helping professions you have a *duty of care* which often remains implicit in formal contracts but is nevertheless fundamental and precious. A lot of damage may ensue if this core principle is violated, precisely because the abuse happens within a helping relationship, which will have been assumed to be safe and exclusively serving the client.

10.3 A professional stance in the here and now

Those helping professions that make use of the relationship itself (e.g. social work, psychotherapy, personal development and coaching, pastoral care) involve the practitioner more fully and cannot avoid making use of the "present moment" in interaction as well.

Only in the present moment can the incommensurability of autonomy and heteronomy models of helping be resolved, because in the present moment "I" and the "Other" share in equal measure, and when we look at what is happening between us we bring together objective and subjective accounts. An observation made in the moment about what is happening in the moment is both objective and subjective in nature: the observation is measurable and falsifiable as it can be checked by the other(s). After all, the evidence is right in front of them, in the present moment. At the same time the observation is highly subjective coming from only one of the participants in the moment.

As a professional in helping relationships where the relationship itself is crucial for the outcome, for example, through the quality and encouragement of the working alliance, it is worth studying your own "present moment" through reflection and meditation. It is worth following your affect, your emotions, and your bodily sensations, as you are sitting with your experience in a helping conversation. There are essentially three reasons why it so important to practice self-knowledge even in the present moment:

1. By studying the present moment you strengthen the working alliance or at least help to make it more explicit. You will be experienced as more present, focused and aware—and in most cases your clients, pupils or patients will prefer you more present rather than less present.

2. By studying the present moment you may be in a position to offer what is called "here and now observations and feedback": hypotheses about what might be going on right now in the relationship. Examples are "I am noticing some pressure here to come up with a solution, I am feeling under pressure right now", "As you tell me this I can tell you are possibly irritated about it, through the way your eyes light up and your jaw stiffens", or "You are telling me how your pupils often get distracted and start fidgeting or doing other things; I have to confess I am feeling the same need as I have been listening for a while and you are giving me a lot of detail. I am not clear what you want us to work with among all that detail". It is worth recalling the last time you received "here and now feedback", that is, when a friend, a colleague or your partner pointed something out to you about how you came across in that very moment. Chances are that this was quite powerful feedback and that it got you thinking about yourself. Here and now observations have this quality of being rather powerful, as they are often based on inescapable evidence, and it is quite hard to dismiss or avoid any fresh thinking, as that would mean changing the subject of the conversation completely. It is quite a responsibility as well to give such observations, and requires some courage, as they are so pertinent and even bordering on being intrusive and rude. Yet at the same time they do help your counterpart to reconsider their conception of themselves in relationship.

3. By studying the present moment you may notice or help your counterpart to change something in their stance or behaviour right now, here in the room with you. Such conscious changes in the here and now are known to be quite impactful and more easily repeated "out there" in your counterpart's life and work with others. So from here-and-now observations may come here-and-now conscious changes that tend to have real, measurable consequences. They often are the moments that your clients will come back to in the next sessions—the moments when something different happened between you and them.

The ability to work in the moment in such a way, deepening the alliance, noticing moments of interaction and facilitating new experiments, is what is called *relational practice* or relationality. When successful a micro-integration takes place which is both an integration at the level of the person and at the level of the profession, because person and profession come together in the "here and now" of helping conversations.

Case example: supervision as a professional lifeline

Kurt is a participant in an academic qualification programme that he has decided to begin after practising in the profession already for a number of years, thanks to his commercial acumen. He sees himself as rather successful, and yet he has agonising qualms as well about his practice and his professionalism. He does experience himself as an impostor every time he reflects about his career and professional identity, as he is essentially working in this profession without a license or qualification. After exploring alternative qualifications on the internet and ruminating for a while about which one would be best for him, Kurt has chosen for this programme at the Almamater University.

He arrives very keen to learn. At the same time he is also tense because of meeting a new group in a new environment, and unsure whether he needs to put himself through all of this. On meeting the group he finds himself rather different from the others: most other delegates are older than him, they are from a different part of the country, and they seem to understand more about Almamater courses. His first year is full of disappointment for him, regarding the low level of student services, the poor quality of teaching, the "irrelevant" assignments he is being asked to do, and the collaboration with his tutor who does not seem to understand what he has written. At the end of the year there is a practice examination which he dramatically fails and he also comes into more open conflict: once or twice with the lunchroom staff and later also with his examiners at the oral exam. His tutor tells him that he should engage in regular therapy for himself during his stay on the remainder of the programme, and the examiners tell him that they want no further meetings with him as the discussions about his low marks were becoming so bitter and acrimonious.

Kurt feels increasingly isolated also from his peers. Once he walks out of his class mid-session because he feels he cannot contain his emotions and he finds himself wandering on a long and random walk through town. Fortunately, later on the same day the teacher helps him in a gentle way to get back into class, and he does not feel too ashamed or humiliated. After much deliberation, also with his wife and other family members, he decides not to take up that suggestion of therapy but to ask for 10 individual sessions of supervision with his favourite teacher, who agrees with this idea.

Unbeknownst to him by this time the faculty on his course is pretty much split in the middle in terms of how to "manage" Kurt on the programme. Some members of faculty advise to remove him from further training or to make the weekly individual therapy recommendation conditional to his progression on the programme. Other faculty members, who haven't met Kurt, are intrigued and ask questions about what is going on, or emphasise the "duty of care" that the whole programme has towards Kurt. In the end the individual supervision sessions with one member of faculty bear fruit. They provide Kurt with a lifeline and allow him to think through his relationships with faculty. Moreover, he brings up many of his commercial clients in supervision, and as it turns out some of these clients present with rather serious psychopathology. He finally receives—in his view—some real practical learning that he can use in his work. Over time he also receives help from his supervisor with his next assignment, which he is able to pass. After much doubt and hesitation, he is even able to go back to some of the Almamater employees (support staff and faculty) that he has so upset in the past. The supervisor keeps bringing up what she calls Kurt's "eccentricity", the fact that he comes across as different from the rest of his peer group or is attached to being different, and also names his isolation and possible loneliness on the course. The supervisor even calls out Kurt's resentment, his hostility towards the institution that is making learning so hard for him. The supervisor then speaks about Kurt's possible hostility towards herself. She uses Kurt's silences or stubbornness when she as a supervisor raises something awkward about the present moment, as illustrations of what she is trying to understand. In all of this Kurt consistently feels that his supervisor is on his side, so he is able to look into his own hostility. He feels the supervisor believes in him and has his best interests at heart, so he never misses a session and keeps "forking out the incredibly high fee", as he calls it, from his personal account.

Later and for the rest of his career Kurt looks back on the Almamater training programme with great satisfaction, gratitude, and pride, as a turning point not just in his professional identity but also in terms of his self-image and family relationships. One wonders what would have happened to Kurt on this programme if he had not received what he regarded as helpful supervision.

11 Links between person and profession

The main aim of supervision is to forge or reinforce productive links between person and profession. In Chapter 9 we focused on the person, in Chapter 10 on the profession. Here, we take another look at the links between the two. We consider three different aspects: the personal process of development towards the profession; learning for, in and from the profession; professional practice itself, with attention to the various forms of support available to practitioners.

11.1 Professional socialisation

Probably every practitioner in the helping profession has asked or will ask herself at some stage how she ended up choosing their profession. How and why did you become the person you are now? Which ideals, insights, values, (missed) opportunities, or personal circumstances motivated you to take up this profession? Why do you want to make yourself available for it (see also section 9.2)? Self-knowledge can help you to gain a better understanding of others, so these are good questions to ask.

Socialisation is embedded in the interconnectedness of person and profession, a link so strong that we are often unaware of it. We live our social existence in two dimensions: on the one hand, we locate ourselves in the given situation and allow ourselves to be determined by where we are; on the other hand, we take responsibility for the situation and work towards change. In other words, our lives are lived for us but we also shape our lives ourselves by taking our fate into our own hands.

Socialisation is the process by which an individual learns to become a member of society. All kinds of learning processes form part of socialisation, teaching the person the knowledge, standards, and skills that are expected of them as a member of society. In this sense, socialisation is a sort of induction process and functions as a stabiliser in an existing societal context of social systems.

There is also another side to socialisation. Individuals are never a member of just one social system but belong to several at the same time and in succession (e.g. associations such as the family, community, school, work, leisure activities, religious community). Each of these systems has its own ideas, values, standards, and rules of behaviour. As a result, we are confronted with (often wide-ranging) differences between subsystems in the society in which we live. Such confrontation gives rise to critical questions and the need to change something. Socialisation is therefore both a stabilising influence and an engine for change.

Forms of socialisation

Socialisation can be differentiated into three forms: primary socialisation, secondary socialisation, and professional socialisation. These are examined in turn below.

a. Primary socialisation

Children and young people learn to differentiate at an early age, in their primary environment (family or other community). The first difference they experience is the distinction between "I" (or "me") and "you": the experience that there is another person who also calls themself "I" but is not me. In the next stage, they discover the difference between "we" and "they", or "us" and "them": the experience that others think, feel, want and act differently than we do, and "we" find that pretty strange at first. In primary socialisation, we internalise the heritage passed down to us by our social environment. In other words, we adopt its views, ways of life, manners and standards of behaviour and make them so much our own that we (come to) recognise them as part of ourselves.

b. Secondary socialisation

This induction process continues in our secondary environment (primary and secondary education, work, leisure activities, mass media, etc.). The intellectual heritage we gained "back home" comes with us, and is put to the test, criticised and possibly altered. The new insights, standards, and values we have acquired also become internalised; the old is incorporated into the new and integrated into a growing autonomy.

c. Professional socialisation

Professional socialisation is where you acquire everything that is expected of you as a (future) holder of certain roles and social positions. More specifically, professional socialisation is the process by which the members of a profession pass on their definition of the profession's activities to newcomers. In this learning aimed at developing professional competence, both training and practice play an important role. Newcomers learn to find their own way within the profession, partly with the aid of supervision.

Self-knowledge

In the helping professions, a practitioner's self-knowledge is an important basis for making contact with and developing understanding of the people who rely on them and hope for their understanding. Someone who is aware of their own path in life, their own heritage, the obstacles they face and the pillars on which the whole edifice is founded—such as their parental social environment, gender, educational background, ethnic origin, religion, beliefs, views, health or physical ability—will be more able to open themselves up to the socialisation of others and be aware of the other-ness of the other (section 9.1). What "we" found strange before could now be seen as something to become curious about.

In supervision, (professional) socialisation can be taken as a fact and as a starting point, because it is not the immediate focus. Nevertheless, for the supervisor and any co-supervisees, some information about socialisation may be important because it can help to understand each other better and sooner.

11.2 Learning and facilitation of learning

The key function of supervision is to facilitate learning aimed at developing professional competence, and to do so in a specific way and with a particular emphasis. In the following section we look at an aspect that we have not touched on previously: what *is* learning in the first place? How do we learn what we need to learn? What is facilitated learning, of which supervision is just one form?

Forms of learning

In section 11.1 we saw that learning occurs in all three dimensions of socialisation. In the beginning, children learn about their world and themselves mainly through their experiences with people, nature, and things. This continues in the next stage where this purely "experiential" learning is supplemented with cognitive knowledge acquisition. This happens mainly via language: learning in education and information from the mass media (television, radio, newspapers, internet). When we reach the stage of familiarising ourselves with a profession or occupation, both forms of learning become the focus of renewed attention, perhaps more consciously and hopefully in alignment with each other. Theory and practice are linked in professional training, yet the work itself can be learned only by actively pursuing the profession, that is, by doing the job and gaining experience in practice.

Concepts of learning

Education experts have different views on what is meant by learning. For the purposes of this book we can define learning as a process of cognitive reorganisation that has consequences for someone's thoughts, feelings, wishes and actions. Here is a way to operationalise "learning" that does not refer to the (invisible) inner world of the learner, which remains inaccessible to an observer (De Haan, 2005):

- *Learning*: a process in which *knowledge* is created by the transformation of experience.
- *Knowledge*: human knowledge (perceptions, cognitions, skills, attitudes) is an irreversible change in potential actions.

This includes our exploration of the world, but also our everyday learning at school. In education we often learn two things at the same time in a way that makes them hard to distinguish:

1. *Beliefs*: crediting, having faith in something, accepting it as (potentially) true (as in, what do I hold true?).
2. *Values*: principles, positive or negative assessments, likes and dislikes (as in, what do I think of it?).

Values are learned through a process of identification with a person, group, vision, religion, belief system, etc. To some degree positive identifications are necessary for any cognitive reorganisation, that is, for learning both *beliefs* and *values*. A learning process is therefore quite radical and hopefully promotes coherence between thoughts, feelings, wishes, and actions (in supervision terms this is called *integration*, see section 6.1). In general education the focus on coherence and integration is not yet widely accepted and the emphasis may be too strongly on the acquisition of beliefs at the expense of the honing of (personal) values.

Autonomy learning

Many educational institutions implicitly adhere to an "autonomy" model of learning and teaching where the emphasis is on rational models and "objective" truths.

An example of such an "autonomy" approach to learning is cognitive learning theory, which holds that intentional action is based on knowledge and intellectual skills and can be traced to the philosophies of John Watson and Robert Gagné. Gagné's (1975) theory can be summarised as follows: information is absorbed, processed, and stored in the memory for later use. The memory is divided into a working memory (for the short term) and a sort of memory reservoir (long term):

- The *short-term memory*: the information we pay heed to (attention is selective) ends up here. The symbols we perceive (e.g. letters) are recognised: a combination of letters is recognised as a word, a combination of words as a sentence, a combination of sentences as a message. The symbols are assigned a value: classed as likes or dislikes; coded (organised in a particular way) and stored in the memory.
- The *long-term memory*: this is where the coded information ends up, to be stored for later use. This information can be retrieved with the help of clues or signals. To facilitate retrieval, a direct or indirect link must have been made between coding and clues in the first stage, for instance by observing, listening, seeing, and so on, consciously and with purpose.

To stimulate the learning process, which takes place largely in the working memory, learning objectives should intentionally be kept to the fore when selecting information obtained from observations. They can then act as clues during the feedback process (reflection) with the retrieval of relevant information from the long-term memory. Continual measurement against learning objectives can guide a learning process in a problem-oriented manner and thereby make it more effective. Also, different instructional conditions are likely to bring about different types of cognitive learning, so it is important to adapt the learning process to the particular knowledge that needs to be "built" in the mind of the learner.

Heteronomy learning

In supervision the kind of rational, linear learning described above may be important but it is certainly not the only form of learning. There is also an emphasis on the more personal, "subjective" learning. To understand a "heteronomy" approach to learning it is important to go back to our unique personal experiences, and to see how we could learn something with relevance for ourselves, for example, a much-needed shift in values or self-image.

A good way to link learning directly to specific personal experiences is to make use of the theory espoused by David Kolb (1984), which sees learning as an individual problem-solving process. The starting point here is not cognition but experience. Kolb's ideas on experiential learning can be summed up as follows: "experiential learning is a process in which knowledge is created through the transformation of experience", with five characteristics:

1. Learning is a spiral process in which knowledge is continually derived from, judged against and altered by a person's experiences. An experience is the assigning of meaning to the things that happen to you (see section 3.1); it can be broken down into internal experience (subjective) and external experience (objective).
2. Learning involves transactions, an interaction between you as a person and those around you. For example, a supervisee who is given a task and is deemed able to carry it out based on her or his existing expertise.
3. Learning is also a holistic process of alignment with "the world". People need to relate to (adopt an attitude towards) tasks posed by those around them and by life in general. A learning process encourages the integration of observations, thoughts, feelings, and actions.
4. The learning process requires resolution of conflicts between opposing ways of aligning with the world. New insights or skills can clash with old ones; a solution has to be found. In addition, there

is usually a tension between the desire to change and resistance to change.

5. Learning processes are focused on knowledge acquisition. Functional knowledge stems from the interaction between the knowledge base in a particular (professional) culture and the personal knowledge already acquired from experience.

Kolb's theory can be adapted well to forms of peer learning (De Haan, 2005), and also to supervision when viewed as a process of experiential learning which supports the independent functioning of a practitioner. For learning to take place on the basis of experience you need to:

- First and foremost, *notice* your experience and observe it in a rich and deep way;
- Be able to *link* your own actions with what you notice and what feelings the experience has triggered within you;
- Understand your *stance* and the attitude that has led you to this experience and your behaviour in it;
- Understand what you *want* now as a result of the experience;
- *Plan* alternative ways of achieving what you wish to achieve;
- Remain aware of how all of this relates to the demands of good professional *practice*;
- *Sensitise* yourself to new experiences on the basis of your planned actions.

Learning in supervision

Learning in supervision draws on both autonomy and heteronomy models of learning; for example, there are two ways in which you can approach your supervisor in the interests of your learning:

1. Making your supervisor into a "role model" or "identification-based learning": you as a supervisee are focused on your connections with the supervisor and you readily adopt the latter's insights and actions;
2. Critically observing your supervisor as a "benchmark" for learning, or "oppositional learning": you as a supervisee are focused on emphasising differences from the supervisor and are less likely to

adopt anything from the latter yet you are learning through critical appraisal of the other person.

Here we see again the distinction between placing the other at the centre of a learning process and placing oneself at the centre, in a different guise. In the former (which is arguably a heteronomy approach), a learning problem can emerge due to over-dependence on the supervisor. But in the latter (arguably an autonomy approach), learning can be inhibited by the supervisee closing off to the supervisor's influence.

Goal-oriented learning is certainly a useful concept in supervision. However, it requires the supervisee's learning objectives to be known (precisely enough) in advance, which is not usually possible in supervision. It is often the case that learning goals only emerge, crystallise, and evolve during the supervision process itself. However, the supervisor does keep an eye on the initially agreed, general objectives and may use them to guide the supervisee's unmapped path of discovery.

Experiential learning as a *problem-solving process*, as Kolb (1984) sees it, proves very useful in supervision practice, precisely because supervision is so oriented towards experience and practice. The learning process consists of four transitions, known as "Kolb's learning cycle":

1. Concrete *experience*: something happening in practice, here and now.
2. Reviewing events and observations: reaping the benefits of *reflection*.
3. Abstract *conceptualisation* and generalisation based on *analysis*.
4. Active *experimentation* or trying out what you have learned in your *practice*. This leads to new experience, and so on.

Where you start out on the cycle does not really matter (this also depends on your personal learning and working preferences), but it *is* important to keep trying to "close the loop". By doing so, you learn to expand your own possibilities and to make your learning process effective. For example, a "doer" could set a personal objective of learning to reflect more effectively, and a "thinker" could aim to be bolder about taking decisions and trying things out in practice. For more information on how to apply Kolb's model on professional practice-related learning, see De Haan (2005).

Facilitated learning

At the start of this section, supervision was described as a form of facilitated learning. Learning methods include:

- Self-study: learning without help from others, for example, by reading or reflective journaling.
- Learning with help from others: mutual learning by helping or supporting each other (in a learning or study group).
- Facilitated learning: learning based on a division of roles between learning and facilitating (student and facilitator).

Supervision is a facilitated learning situation in which the positions of supervisor and supervisee are clearly differentiated. The supervisee comes to supervision to learn, and the supervisor helps. At the same time there are elements of mutual learning as the supervisor is also testing hypotheses and learning something new. And there are elements of self-study, particularly in the preparation for supervision or in the review and implementation afterwards.

Forms of facilitated learning processes are associated with different concepts of learning. This can lead to a preference for:

- The *linear form*: the various stages of learning are undertaken in a chronological sequence; returning to a previous stage is seen as a departure.
- The *spiral form*: again, there is a staged sequence but returning to a previous stage is undertaken with more development or expansion.
- The *cyclical form*: a linear sequence is abandoned; the learning process moves to and fro between the different stages but nevertheless progresses.

Learning conditions and learning styles

There are two core roles supporting learning in supervision, that of the supervisee and that of the supervisor:

- The *supervisor* attempts to encourage the supervisee's learning based on her personal idea of facilitated learning. Supervisors also take care of the learning conditions within supervision, not only by laying down clear ground rules (see Chapter 2) but also by making space for new insights and monitoring space for learning and change.

- The *supervisee* comes to learn, but does so based on his own capabilities and ambivalences, and the particular way in which he learns, his personal learning style (see section 5.3, and the concepts of learning and Kolb's "learning cycle" described above).

Learning from experience contrasts with learning from information. In the latter, the learning material is contributed from the outside (via teachers, literature, etc.). In supervision, the supervisee herself supplies the learning material by contributing her own experience (the "work contribution"). As the supervisee's learning facilitator, the supervisor has goals to achieve and resources to use in processing that learning material together with the supervisee. Supervisors sometimes apply their own emphasis in this facilitated learning, for example, one of the following (compare the seven-eyed model in Hawkins & Shohet, 2006):

- emphasis on the supervisee's *person* and personal history, with a strong focus on the latter's internal experiences (the supervisee's internal narrative);
- emphasis on the supervisee's *work*, with a strong focus on the supervisee's clients, the contextual field and work situation (the contextual narrative);
- emphasis on the combination of *person and profession*, with equal focus on subjective aspects of the person and objective aspects of the work (the integration or socialisation narrative);
- emphasis on a particular *method*, with a greater focus on the method of learning or working than on the areas mentioned above (the instrumental narrative);
- emphasis on the supervisor's *person*, with a strong focus on the supervisor's internal experience and affect (the supervisor's internal narrative);
- emphasis on the *parallel process* occurring between the work combination (the supervisee with others at work) and this supervision combination (the underlying counter/transference or attachment narrative).

However, the most striking feature of all forms and nuances of learning in supervision is that supervision makes conscious use of a method which, although unrecognised at the time, has already proved effective in your primary socialisation (section 11.1), that is, learning from your experiences.

For supervision, a specific feature is that those experiences are linked to profession and practice. Supervision learning takes place with awareness, purposefully, systematically and procedurally (section 3.1); the process serves as a means towards achieving particular (personal and functional) learning objectives.

11.3 Working and work support

Learning for the purposes of a profession is never complete as there is always more to learn, but it can be terminated (for the time being and somewhat prematurely) once you have completed your professional training. However, this ending does not usually apply to learning in and from professional practice. If supervision has taught you to learn from your own experience in practice, that is, to use that experience to make good progress, you are often able (initially) to continue your personal learning process independently and through self-supervision. If, after a while, you feel a need to review and/or update your professional practice, you might consider undergoing another period of supervision. Apart from training supervision, there are several other ways to contract for supervision, for example, via your professional (care, consulting) institution or by commissioning it yourself (section 1.2).

In the following pages we highlight some other forms of in-post learning. Peer consultation is similar to supervision due to its focus on continued learning in and from your practice. In the other forms, the primary goal is not so much learning but rather functioning in the work setting.

Continuing professional development (CPD)

After their initial professional training, sometimes followed by refresher courses or other further training, workers in the helping professions can take up various forms of continuing professional development. Special in-service training courses or CPD events are organised in many professional settings. These programmes focus on particular aspects of professional practice and are intended to broaden your skill base or improve the quality of the work. The serious practitioner is also expected to keep up to date with developments in the profession and in the wider field of practice. This is vital, especially in the present-day context, which is subject to so many changes. Keeping abreast of specialist literature can play an important role in this, and is often a professional requirement.

Peer consultation or action learning

A well-known form of CPD in professional practice is action learning or peer consultation, which can be seen as a variant of supervision. Like supervision, peer consultation is a form of "learning with help from others" (De Haan, 2005). A peer-consultation group is a gathering of colleagues who have agreed on what and how they want to learn from each other and meet regularly over a given period without a supervisor. In some cases they may use a peer consultation facilitator or group supervisor for a while to start them off—or later on, for example, to nurture more challenging feedback.

Peer consultation can be a good way to continue learning for your profession in a personalised way (section 1.3). This is especially true for practitioners who already have experience of supervision and have a common basis for a shared learning process in combination with working in practice.

In our view, peer consultation cannot really replace supervision: supervision brings added value in the shape of the independent views of a supervisor and the fact that facilitated learning in supervision is not mutual but is wholly for the supervisee's benefit. However, regular peer consultation can reduce the required frequency of supervision.

Work support and learning

Training and CPD are focused on the (future) practitioner's learning. Various forms of work support are geared to what the practitioner already knows and can do, with the goal of utilising that knowledge or maximising that ability. These are forms of learning inside the workplace and inside your job or role, "*in situ*". You can certainly learn from this, but learning tends to be an incidental outcome rather than the primary goal of work support. Learning changes something in the competence of the worker himself, while support is focused on the work and the performance of the worker's tasks (which may need to be improved). Some well-known forms of work support which enjoy a certain reputation and are (or may be) useful for many are work supervision, administrative supervision, and learning on the job.

Practice supervision

Practice supervision is intended for trainees who as part of their professional training are undertaking a placement with a professional care institution and being supervised by a professional from that institution. This is a specific form of work supervision, focused on the combination of working and learning and the tensions it can evoke. The practice supervisor (often the institution's work supervisor) therefore bears a dual responsibility: making sure the work is done properly and within requirements, and facilitating learning for the trainee. In practice, work supervision can be as useful to the trainee as other forms of (off-line) supervision, and is often a rich context for learning, provided the supervisor takes the trainee's learning and development to heart and does not focus only on what clients/patients might need from the supervisee.

Work supervision

Work supervision is focused on implementing the policy of the institution or organisation and on supporting employees in their work. Work supervision is not focused on the worker's learning, although learning and gaining competence can certainly be an outcome. The work supervisor has a managerial responsibility and also has various (potentially conflicting) tasks to support professionals doing their job. In some sectors such as nursing and other caring professions, work supervision is called "clinical supervision". Terms such as "in-post training" and "mentoring" are also used, although it is debatable whether these forms of supervision correspond entirely to "work supervision".

Consultation

Consultation is a form of work support that offers occasional help with a work problem. This is about "problem solving in professional practice", on an *ad hoc* basis. Such help can also be sought repeatedly from the same consultation giver. The initiative always lies with the requester, who remains responsible for dealing with the problem concerned. This focus on *problem solving* is a clear difference compared with supervision (although learning for professional development can again be an indirect consequence of consultation).

Forms of consultation between colleagues are:

- The *consult*: the worker seeks advice from a colleague who special-ises in a particular field or is more experienced than the requester. Requester and giver can be from the same profession but this is often not the case (e.g. a GP consulting a psychologist). A consult is often a one-off, *ad hoc* occurrence.
- *Peer review* (De Haan, 2005): this is about mutual help between col-leagues, which can go beyond seeking or giving advice on a specific problem. Colleagues can help each other to clarify specific isolated or recurring problems in their work, and then work together to find the right approach. However, peer review remains confined to clarify-ing, monitoring, and solving problems in a specific work situation. Sometimes (for example, in partnerships), peer review can replace direct managerial relationships in the helping professions and thus may include performance review and appraisals.

The main difference between *peer review* and *peer consultation* lies in their objectives. Peer consultation is about learning from and within the pro-fession as a group of colleagues; peer review focuses on clarification, advice, assistance, assessment, and evaluation in relation to progress or specific work problems (De Haan, 2005).

Another difference is that, in peer consultation and action learning, colleagues learn from each other, that is, their learning is mutual and they are equal in that respect. On the other hand, consultation and peer review involve an asymmetry of roles: a worker with a problem seeks advice from or appeals to someone with more expertise in the particu-lar field. This can also happen in the context of peer consultation, of course, but is usually reversed there after a while.

Case example of professional socialisation

Gloria was a senior recruiter and line manager in her firm, when she decided to branch out and develop herself as a management-development consultant. Over the course of some five years, and with much help from the professional qualification courses she attended and her supervisors, she gradually established her new professional identity and reputation.

In fact, Gloria and her individual supervisor Aretha noticed that this went better for her one-to-one work than when it came to working with groups

---

and teams. Her one-to-one work consisted of a continuation of recruitment assignments and a growing amount of executive coaching. With teams she admitted to feeling really shy and overwhelmed, and even when work was offered to her she named others or came up with 'ethical' concerns that led to her not accepting those assignments. In such cases Gloria would say things like, "I am already doing some individual coaching for this organisation; so I think it would be good if you could ask someone else for this team facilitation".

It transpired that her personal journey to grow into "team consulting" work remained one of Gloria's main objectives in supervision, for at least another five years. She realised that she had not worked much with teams before and that this felt really new for her. She developed both a strong attachment with and a somewhat distorted image of Aretha, whom she imagined was very confident and proficient with all sorts of challenging teams and boards. Gloria's mixed feelings made it sometimes hard to reflect together with Aretha as she for example, gave her direct questions such as "what would you do here, Aretha?" She also struggled to accept Aretha's ideas perhaps because some hidden envy or competition was playing out. Moreover, Gloria's first two team assignments, in the area of "action learning", were not successful, and she spoke about them with embarrassment. It was very difficult to reflect afterwards with Aretha about what might have worked better and to consider what "mistakes" (as Gloria insisted on calling them) Gloria might have made.

Yet Gloria persisted and she started taking on some "low-hanging fruit": team assignments that were suggested to her by her otherwise impressed sponsors and clients of individual-coaching work, and she participated in a few group-dynamics conferences. Slowly she turned the situation around and started working more and more with teams, often in a pair with a close colleague, and usually while scrupulously going through all the details and potential outcomes with Aretha in supervision. She became more and more articulate in naming her expertise, her own particular cross between recruitment, individual, and team coaching. In the end she could also explain very well why she did not take on facilitation, educational, and organisational-development duties. All of this made sure that she had a clear niche in the marketplace and that her small company continued to flourish.

12 The importance of understanding in supervision

A single connecting theme runs through everything that has to do with a person's development towards gaining or improving professional competence, and that theme is *awareness*. Professional workers are generally expected to know the hows, whys, and wherefores before making a decision and taking action in practice.

For the helping professions, the importance of self-knowledge is closely bound up with understanding of others and skilful provision of services. An essential condition in this respect is having and gaining awareness of what is happening in and around yourself. To achieve this, you need to have strong powers of observation and analysis, and the ability to explore a set of circumstances or a person's situation. Intuition, empathy, and warmth with sympathy are certainly essential, but you also have to employ your thinking and analysis to come to a professional view. Here are some exercises to stimulate your skills of analysis and understanding.

12.1 Self-understanding—a reflective assignment

Following the comments on socialisation in section 11.1, we can take another look at how your own history influenced (and continues to influence) the person you have become. How self-aware are you? How do you connect with your own feelings? How do you deal with fresh experiences? Look in the mirror and talk to yourself. Ask questions such as:

- What do my social origins have to do with my current choice of profession and way of working? How was this influenced by my learning history and educational background?
- To what extent were there any positive or negative effects of gender socialisation, of "induction" as a man or woman? Effects of societal or educational socialisation?
- Which "direction-setting views" (grand "theories of man"; section 10.1) helped or hindered me in developing my own ideas?
- Which values matter to me at present, and why?
- To what extent can I identify and utilise my own feelings? Can I link (practical) experiences to myself? How do I handle myself in the midst of new and surprising experiences?

- Where do my skills still fall short? What am I already (fairly) good at? How do I relate to others? What are my main relational models that I take from one client to the next?

12.2 Understanding yourself in your practice

There are various ways to resolve personal and interpersonal problems, but not all of them are equally effective. Sometimes "guesswork" succeeds but it can also go completely wrong: when you are "barking up the wrong tree". Then your well-meaning guesswork and intuition could even compound your issue at hand. There are other ways to move from a current (problematic) situation to a more desirable one. One of these is the problem-solving method (De Haan, 2005).

The problem-solving method has four distinct steps. Why not take a current challenge or issue in your professional practice and apply this method to the issue, following the steps below? So before you read on, formulate a problem that has relevance for you at this present moment!

1. Exploring the problem

Who has the problem, and with what or whom? What does the problem consist of (main problem, additional issues)? Who is most affected by the problem or a sub-issue: you, the person concerned (your client or patient?), family, care provider(s), or who else? Why? Which solution seems to be most desirable, for whom and/or for which problem?

2. Formulating goals

What would be the best outcome for you? Are there any other possible outcomes that would be "good enough" for you? Who wants to implement which solution? Are there any realistic alternatives? If so, what are they? How can they be achieved, when and by whom?

3. Planning and implementation

How much time do people think they will need to achieve their final goal? What pace or schedule is necessary or desirable: do we take the motorway or the scenic route? What methods, resources and aids are available? And who does what and by when?

4. Review and evaluation

Step back for a moment and consider what this exercise and this method has brought you. You might also look at your issue and the method with the help of the extra "Balint" step, named after the Hungarian psychoanalyst Michael Balint (see De Haan, 2005): *"What in my way of choosing the problem today, bringing it to this exercise, and going through the exercise, is also relevant for the problem itself?"* In other words, how is the "here and now" of me going through these steps relevant for my problem and its potential solution? Little things of seemingly no relevance may be important here; for example, how have you chosen the "problem"? Have you chosen "safely"? Have you chosen something that you already ruminate about a lot? Have you chosen something that has already been largely resolved or laid to rest? Have you hesitated? Have you resisted doing this or some of this? Have you paused at any point? Have you written anything down? What have you chosen to write down and why, do you think? Have you felt emotional at any point? Why do you have this problem in the first place? What has been your own role in causing or prolonging it? These are all here and now questions that you may have steered away from in the answering of the open questions above, but that may nevertheless be relevant.

At the very end, ask yourself what you are going to do now with what you have learned during this exercise, and write down a few actions or intentions.

Case example: understanding emerges over time and may even strike like lightning

Elaine is a psychotherapist with many years' experience. Her children are now about to leave the house and so Elaine has increased her contract as well as engaging in further qualifications and supervision. During the last year, during these learning activities, she has discovered herself making more contact with her own anxieties. She also understood much more about her choices for entering this profession originally, and about the difficulties she has experienced over the years. She recognises in her own early childhood a degree of neglect and how she was forced by circumstances to learn to look after herself at a very early age. She remembers also how for a period she became the confidante of one of her parents, as they were experiencing turbulence in their marriage.

Having recognised these things and beginning to come to terms with them, Elaine makes an interesting discovery in her practice, which she brings to supervision repeatedly. Her newer patients appear to be much more emotional with her than those that came before: they are often distressed and overwhelm her with their vulnerabilities and their claims for help.

Elaine starts working through these cases during consecutive supervision sessions. The way she would sum it up is: as she recently became more vulnerable her patients have also become more fragile. She is finding her work more difficult and needs more supervision to determine how to respond to the heightened distress, disappointments and demands. She finds herself very cautiously, delicately and gently working with quite emotional patients. Her main query in several supervision sessions is that she does not really "name" or "raise" with her patients what she picks up emotionally, and her supervisor agrees. Elaine is keeping her sensibility inside herself.

She starts working with her supervisor to become more firm, matter of fact, robust and containing; the way she always used to be, but hopefully at the deeper emotional level required at the moment.

One session Elaine talks through how she wants to work with "backbone and heart" and particularly develop the former: her inner strength. She goes through a number of case examples. When she and her supervisor look back on the supervision session itself she suddenly feels concerned about her supervisor. "And how are you, are you all right?", she asks with some anxiety. At that point—and only thanks to the fact that her supervisor stops in her tracks and raises her eyes—Elaine realises how she is now approaching her supervisor as if she were the parent who always wanted to confide in her. Something clicks for her about how the past is still with her and she feels encouraged to be a lot more robust with her "fragile" patients. This works out very well in her practice and even in working with some of her colleagues in the hospital where she works.

NOTES

Introduction

1. Notable exceptions are *On Becoming a Supervisee* by Carroll & Gilbert (2005) and *Getting the Most from Supervision* by Dunnett, Jesper, O'Donnell, & Vallance (2013). More recent guides for supervisors also focus more explicitly on the supervisee. See for example chapter three of *Supervision in Action* by De Haan (2012).
2. This book has had eight editions in Holland over a twenty-five-year period, that is, since 1991.

2

1. The majority of professional associations have their own ethical codes that are generally available on their websites. As an example please find the Ashridge code of conduct for supervisors in Appendix B. Recently, initiatives have been launched to harmonise ethical principles and supervisor competency requirements within Europe, for example within the European Mentoring & Coaching Council (EMCC) and within ECVision, a European Union project.
2. However, there are also some more promising findings. In a recent large-scale survey of coaching supervisees 518 responses were received

from 356 female and 162 male coaches (De Haan, 2016). Statistical properties of the responses were computed and two-sample t-tests were conducted to look at the influence of gender, age, experience, nationality, amount, and nature of supervision taken (ratios between group and individual supervision) on the satisfaction and trust scores. The results show that these experienced coaches are considerably more safe, satisfied, and trusting of their supervisor than was found in comparable research in counselling and psychotherapy. Significant differences were found in the appreciation of supervision by men and women, and also with supervisee age and relative exposure to supervision:

- Women are significantly more open in supervision and as a result receive more help with their most concerning episodes.
- Older coaches are also more open than younger ones in terms of bringing their most concerning episodes; and moreover they report higher levels of trust in their supervisor.
- More experienced coaches report higher levels of trust in their supervisor.
- Taking more supervision also correlates with openness and receiving help with their most concerning episodes.
- Coaches who take relatively more individual than group supervision achieve slightly higher levels of satisfaction and trust with their supervisors.

At least from the perspective of this sample of relatively senior coaches, it seems that where coaches self-select and contract with their supervisors and pay supervision out of the proceeds of their own practice, highly trusting and satisfactory relationships with supervisors are emerging, although even in this study there were still instances of lack of trust and safety.

3

1. However, in order to have enough time for each supervisee, a supervisor will need at the very minimum a quarter-day (around two hours) for a group of up to four participants and at least a half-day for a group of up to eight, unless the group meets as regularly as once a week.

5

1. In contrast to many of the other helping professions where it is unethical to have other relationships after the functional relationship ends, this same phenomenon is actually in many cases unavoidable—and quite manageable—in supervision, where a peer-to-peer relationship remains after ending. However, it is still important to mark and negotiate the transition to other ways of working together when a supervisory journey ends.

9

1. For example, professional associations for supervisors include AOCS in the United Kingdom, LVSC in the Netherlands, ANSE in large parts of Europe and AAOS in Australia and Asia.

GLOSSARY OF TERMS

*indicates a term also found in this Glossary.

Attitude: a way of thinking or feeling about something.
Authority: a legitimised power* derived from a profession or post.
Autonomy learning and autonomy ethics: "the thinking person surveys the world and makes herself the norm of reality" (in contrast to "heteronomy learning"*).

continuing professional development (CPD): ongoing learning for experienced practitioners designed to (1) keep practitioners fresh and susceptible to experience; (2) help practitioners learn from their experiences in their particular helping profession; and (3) inspire and instruct practitioners with new and relevant learning.

Experiential learning: learning from concrete experience by means of reflection*.

Functional relationship: a relationship focused on a functional and agreed objective—as is usual in helping relationships* such as those in supervision.

Helping conversations: the subject matter of supervision; supervision addresses professions in which communication and conversations play a major role.

Helping profession: a profession that nurtures personal growth or addresses problems in a person's physical, psychological, intellectual, emotional or spiritual well-being. Examples include medicine, nursing, psychotherapy, psychological counselling, social work, education, coaching, consulting, and ministry.

Helping relationship: a functional relationship* intended to provide a service to a person. More technically, a relationship where "one of the participants intends that there should come about in one or both parties, more appreciation of, more expression of, more functional use of the latent inner resources of the individual" (Rogers, 1961).

Heteronomy learning and heteronomy ethics (also called "diversity thinking and diversity ethics"): "it is not the I who is the norm of knowledge and ethics, but the other who presents herself to me" (in contrast to "autonomy learning"*).

Interaction: communication between people, involving the exchange of information, insight, emotion, and projection among much else.

Learning: a vehicle used by the supervisor in attempting to do their work.

Learning style: the specific, personal way in which someone acquires new knowledge and expertise.

Motivation: a person's motive for doing something, or their readiness to do or allow something.

Objectivism: seeing not just things and events but also people and social relationships as objects, that is, a form of extreme rationalism*.

Parallel process: the idea that supervision combinations* can begin to mirror the relationships they are concerned with; lessons can be drawn from this.

Peer consultation: mutual assistance from colleagues with a view to resolving work-related problems.

Power: the ability to influence another person's behaviour in a particular direction.

Professional identity: identification with a professional group, including belonging, contribution, and difference.

Professional reputation: the way professional identity* is viewed by others in a professional group.

Professional socialisation: the process by which someone is included in a professional group.

Psychological contract: anything that is not specifically laid down in the (supervision) contract*, that is, anything that can give rise to unexpected yet instructive misunderstandings.

Rational: reasonable, considered, focused.

Rationalism: a school of thought in which rationality is valued over emotion, and in which knowledge or truth can be discovered only through reason.

Reflection: looking back, contemplating and seeking the meaning of what has been seen, experienced, thought, or done, in order to find out something new.

Relationship: a temporary or permanent emotional connection between people, in which experiences, insights, and feelings are exchanged.

Socialisation: the process by which someone becomes a member of a community, professional group, or society.

Subjectivism: an extreme focus on aspects of the self in a social context.

Supervisee: a person receiving supervision.

Supervision: a didactic method focused on acquiring greater personal competence with a view to exercising a helping profession*.

> **Peer supervision**: a form of professional development without a supervisor; the aim is to learn together with a pair or group of colleagues.
>
> **Practice supervision**: a specific form of work supervision*, focused on combined working and learning of trainees in an institution.
>
> **Self-supervision**: the process of internalising certain achievements made in supervision over time, enabling the supervisee (sometimes still hearing their supervisor's voice) to navigate through their work issues.

Supervision combination: a supervisor and one or more supervisees matched together in a supervision process.

Supervision contract: an extremely useful tool in coordinating the expectations of supervisee, supervisor and any clients or interested third parties.

Supervision relationship: the quality of collaboration in a supervision combination*, including agreement about goals and tasks of supervision, and mutual affection.

Supervisor: a person giving supervision, after acquiring the necessary competencies and qualifications.

To assess: to judge a person or thing based on comparisons and (assessment) criteria.

To concretise (or make explicit): to make experiences real or specific; to identify in verifiable terms.

To consult: to seek information and/or advice from an expert.

To evaluate: to attribute a substantiated value judgement*.

To generalise: to seek a broad connection between specific facts or individual behaviours.

To integrate: incorporating parts into an organised whole, resulting in a new whole.

To problematise: to take an experience and draw from it a specific learning or work issue that can then be worked on.

To reflect: to look back, contemplate, and seek the meaning of what has been seen, experienced, thought, or done, in order to learn in some way.

Transcript: a verbatim trace of current practice or else a detailed description from memory, in chronological order, written in the form of a play, A: "...", B: "...", A: "...", etc.

Value judgement: assigning a qualitative value based on experience or expertise-based authority.

Work contribution: what the supervisee contributes to supervision, consisting of either general queries about the supervisee's work context and development, or specific experiences in the form of "casework", "cases", or "issues". This can be unrestricted and "live"; it can take the form of a written report, or of a recording, possibly accompanied by a verbatim transcription.

Work supervision: support for employees in a particular profession or post; the focus is on achieving the institution's policy objectives.

APPENDIX A
Structure of a Supervision Contract

Name of supervisee:	....
Name of supervisor:	....
Main purpose of supervision:	....
	....
	....
The supervision will be successful for the supervisee if:	....
	....
	....
The supervision will be successful for the supervisee's clients/patients, colleagues and managers if:	....
	....
	....
The supervision will be successful for the wider societal context of the supervisee's clients/patients if:	....
	....
	....
Role and contribution of the supervisor:	....
	....
	....
Structure, place, frequency and length of sessions:	....
	....
Confidentiality agreements:	....
	....
Review process for outcomes:	....
Testimonials and data protection:	....
Overall term and fee structure:	....
Date and signatures:	....

APPENDIX B
Ashridge's Code of Conduct for Supervisors

Introduction

The purpose of this Code of Conduct is to establish and maintain standards for supervisors and to inform and protect members of the public, their individual clients (supervisees), and organisations seeking their services.

Ethical standards comprise such values as integrity, competence, confidentiality, and responsibility. Ashridge supervisors, in assenting to this Code, accept their responsibility to supervisees, clients of supervisees, colleagues, and Ashridge. The supervisee's interest is paramount, but where supervisors have a conflict of responsibilities they have to use their considered judgement. Therefore the Code of Conduct is a framework within which to work rather than a set of instructions.

General principles

Firstly, we maintain that:

1. Supervisor and supervisee enter into an equal relationship that is used intentionally for the benefit of the supervisee, and in service of the clients of the supervisee.
2. Supervisees ultimately know best what their needs are and can decide for themselves what they do or do not want, both in their private and in their professional lives; supervisees are therefore also responsible for the choices that they make and accountable for their actions.
3. The responsibility of the supervisor is to give the supervisee an opportunity to explore, discover, and clarify ways of working more satisfyingly, effectively and resourcefully.
4. During supervision, the goals, resources, and choices of the supervisee have priority over those of the supervisor. However, ultimately, the supervisor is also endorsing and in some cases "signing off" the supervisee's practice, and so a supervisor's responsibility includes raising any noticeable boundary issues or areas of risk in a supervisee's practice.

Code of Ethics

Issues of responsibility

- Supervisors are responsible for observing the principles embodied in this Code of Conduct.
- Supervisors accept responsibility for encouraging and facilitating the self-development of the supervisee within the supervisee's own network of relationships.
- The supervisor takes account of the developmental level, abilities and needs of the supervisee.
- The supervisor is aware of her own cultural identity and that of the supervisee and of the possible implications for the supervision of any similarities and differences.
- Supervisors are responsible for ensuring that they are not dependent upon relationships with their supervisees for satisfying their own emotional and other needs.

- During supervision the supervisor will not engage in non-supervision relationships, such as friendship, business or sexual relationships with their supervisees. Supervisors are responsible for setting and monitoring the boundaries between working and other relationships, and for making the boundaries as explicit as possible to the supervisee.
- The supervisor will cooperate in the handling of a complaints procedure if a complaint is brought against her, and make sure that reasonable arrangements have been made for professional liability.

Issues of competence

- Supervisors recognise the power inherent in their position: they realise that they can exert considerable influence, both consciously and unconsciously, on their supervisees and possibly also on third parties.
- Supervisors are aware of the limitations both of their supervision and their personal skills and take care not to exceed either. They refer a supervisee to a colleague, if necessary, and maintain a professional network to that end.
- Supervisors commit themselves to training in supervision and undertake ongoing professional development throughout their careers.
- Supervisors seek ways of increasing their professional development and self-awareness.
- Supervisors monitor their supervision work through regular supervision by professionally competent supervisors, and are able to account to individual supervisees, colleagues and client organisations for what they do and why.
- Supervisors monitor the limits of their own competence.
- Supervisors, along with their employers, have a responsibility to themselves and their supervisees to maintain their own effectiveness, resilience, and ability to help clients. They must be able to identify any situation in which their personal resources have become depleted to the extent that they must seek help and/or withdraw from supervision activities, whether temporarily or permanently.

Code of Practice

- This Code of Practice is intended to provide more specific information and guidance in the implementation of the principles embodied in the Code of Ethics.

Management of the work

- Supervisors should inform supervisees as appropriate about their training and qualifications, and the methods they use.
- Supervisors should clarify with supervisees the number and duration of sessions and level of fees. They should also explore a supervisee's own expectations of what is involved in supervision with her.
- Supervisors should gain the supervisee's permission before conferring with other people about the supervisee. All reports about the supervisee to third parties should be shared and worked through with the supervisee first.
- Supervisors should abstain from using any of the information that they have obtained during supervision for their own personal gain or benefit, except in the context of their own development as a supervisor.
- If there is another internal client or sponsor (e.g. a line manager), supervisors must ensure before the supervision starts that all parties have the same information concerning the overall goal and structure of the supervision and the intended working method. The supervision can progress only if there is agreement between them with respect to its goals and structure. If there is any change in the situation or the assignment, the supervisor formally revises the arrangements with all parties.
- Supervisors who become aware of a conflict between their obligations to a supervisee and their obligation to the helping professions (including their "sign-off" or formal endorsement of a supervisee's practice) or an organisation employing them, will make explicit the nature of the loyalties and responsibilities involved.
- In situations where supervisors have a difference of opinion with the supervisee or other involved parties, they will maintain a reasonable attitude and keep dialogue open.

- Supervisors work with supervisees to terminate supervision when the supervisees have received the help they sought, or if it is apparent that supervision is no longer helping them.

Confidentiality

- Supervisors regard all information concerning the supervisee and the supervisee's clients—received directly, indirectly, or from any other source—as confidential. They protect their supervisees and their clients against the use of personal information and against its publication unless this is authorised by the supervisee or required by law.
- Treating information "in confidence" means not revealing it to any other person or through any public medium, except to those whom supervisors rely on for their own confidential support and supervision.
- If supervisors believe that a supervisee could cause danger to others, they will advise the supervisee that they may break confidentiality and take appropriate action to warn individuals or the authorities.

Advertising/public statements

- The supervisor obtains the agreement of the supervisee before using the name of the supervisee's organisation or other information that can identify the supervisee, as a reference.
- Supervisors do not advertise or display an affiliation with an organisation in a manner that falsely implies sponsorship or verification by that organisation.
- Supervisors do not make false, exaggerated or unfounded claims about what supervision will achieve.

REFERENCES

Bordin, H. (1979). The generalizability of the psychoanalytic concept of the working alliance. *Psychotherapy: Theory, Research and Practice, 16*: 252–260.

Carroll, M. & Gilbert, M. (2005). *On Becoming a Supervisee: Creating Learning Partnerships.* London: Vukani.

Casement, P. (2002). *Learning from our Mistakes.* London: Routledge.

Day, A., De Haan, E., Sills, C., Bertie, C. & Blass, E. (2008). Coaches' experience of critical moments in the coaching. *International Coaching Psychology Review, 3*(3): 207–218.

De Haan, E. (2005). *Learning with colleagues: an action guide to action learning.* Basingstoke: Palgrave Macmillan.

De Haan, E. (2012). *Supervision in action: a relational approach to coaching and organisation supervision.* Columbus, MA: McGraw-Hill.

De Haan, E. (2016). Large-scale survey of trust and safety in coaching supervision: some evidence that we are doing it right. *International Coaching Psychology Review* (in press).

Dunnett, A., Jesper, C., O'Donnell, M. & Vallance, K. (2013). *Getting the most from supervision. A guide for counsellors and psychotherapists.* Basingstoke: Palgrave Macmillan.

Erikson, E. H. (1968). *Identity, Youth and Crisis.* New York: Norton.

Foucault, M. (1961). *History of Madness.* J. Murphy & J. Khalfa (Trans.). New York: Routledge, 2006.

141

Gadamer, H.-G. (1975). Hermeneutics and Social Science. *Philosophy and Social Criticism, 2*: 307–316.

Gagné, R. M. (1975). *Essentials of learning for instruction*. Hinsdale, IL: Dryden.

Gray, L. A., Ladany, N., Walker, J. A. & Ancis, J. R. (2001). Psychotherapy trainees' experience of counterproductive events in supervision. *Journal of Counselling Psychology, 48*: 371–383.

Greenson, R. R. (1965). The working alliance and the transference neuroses. *Psychoanalysis Quarterly, 34*: 155–181.

Hawkins, P. & Shohet, R. (2006). *Supervision in the Helping Professions* (3rd edn). Maidenhead: Open University Press.

Heidegger, M. (1927). *Being and Time*. J. Macquarrie & E. Robinson (Trans.). New York: Harper & Row, 1962.

Heron, J. (1975). *Helping the client*. London: Sage.

Kolb, D. A. (1984). *Experiential Learning: experience as the source of learning and development*. Englewood Cliffs, NJ: Prentice Hall.

Leith, S. (2011). *You Talkin' To Me? Rhetoric from Aristotle to Obama*. London: Profile.

Perlman, H. H. (1957). *Social Casework: A Problem-Solving Process*. Chicago, IL: University of Chicago Press.

Rapoport, L. (1954). The use of supervision as a tool in professional development. *British Journal of Psychiatric Social Work, 2*: 66–74.

Rogers, C. R. (1961). *On Becoming a Person: A Therapist's View of Psychotherapy*. London: Constable.

Rousseau, D. M. (1995). *Psychological contracts in organizations—understanding written and unwritten agreements*. Thousand Oaks, CA: Sage.

Van Eemeren, F. H., Grootendorst, R. & Snoeck Henkemans, A. F. (2002). *Argumentation: analysis, evaluation, presentation*. London: Erlbaum.

Watzlawick, P., Beavin, J. & Jackson, D. D. (1967). *Pragmatics of human communication*. New York: Norton.

Wiggins, L., Bird, J., Reilly, C., Atter, A. & De Haan, E. (2014). Reliving the moment: using audio playback in coaching supervision. *Coaching Today*, April: 23–27.

INDEX

Definitions of most terms can be found in the Glossary of Terms, page 129 onwards

Printed in the United States
by Baker & Taylor Publisher Services